CONGRESSIONAL INVESTIGATING COMMITTEES

AMS PRESS
NEW YORK

SERIES XLVII   No. 1

JOHNS HOPKINS UNIVERSITY STUDIES

IN

HISTORICAL AND POLITICAL SCIENCE

Under the Direction of the

Departments of History, Political Economy, and
Political Science

CONGRESSIONAL INVESTIGATING COMMITTEES

BY

MARSHALL EDWARD DIMOCK, Ph. D.

Instructor in Political Science, University of California, (Los Angeles)

BALTIMORE

THE JOHNS HOPKINS PRESS

1929

Reprinted from the edition of 1929, Baltimore

First AMS EDITION published 1971

Manufactured in the United States of America

International Standard Book Number: 0-404-02134-4

Library of Congress Catalog Number: 72-155626

AMS PRESS INC.
NEW YORK, N.Y.   10003

PREFACE

For almost a decade Congressional investigations have held the center of the political stage. The press has recorded, in great detail, the circumstances of the various problems and intrigues which have provided the material for these committees. The practice heretofore has been to treat each investigation as an isolated phenomenon, as a scavenger which suddenly and rather mysteriously comes into existence, and just as speedily vanishes.

An attempt has been made in this study to consider all of the investigations since 1789, and to interpret their aggregate in terms of political cause and effect. In other words, the writer's purpose has been to consider the problem of investigations in relation to the sum total of the processes of the national government.

The material is grouped into seven chapters. The introductory chapter states the significance of the problem in the United States, with reference to the way in which like functions are fulfilled in other modern constitutional governments. The second chapter narrates the English origin and the transference of the power to colonial and state governments. The three following chapters consider the three legislative functions which Congressional investigations help to fulfill, to wit, the membership function, the lawmaking function, and the function of control over the executive departments. The legal and procedural phases are taken up in chapter VI, and the last chapter is given over to appraisal and forecast.

The writer wishes to make grateful acknowledgment for suggestions and criticisms to Professor W. W. Willoughby, Head of the Department of Political Science at The Johns

Hopkins University, to President Frank J. Goodnow, of the Johns Hopkins University, to Mr. W. F. Willoughby, Director of the Bureau of Government Research, Washington, D. C., to Dr. James Hart, of the Department of Political Science, and to my wife, who participated in both the research and the preparation of the manuscript. For the uncorrected errors of fact, reasoning, or language, the writer alone is responsible.

M. E. D.

CONTENTS

vii

CONTENTS

CONGRESSIONAL INVESTIGATING COMMITTEES

CHAPTER I

INTRODUCTORY

Legislatures in Modern Democratic Governments.—Legislative committees of investigation play a part in most of the principal constitutional governments of the present day. In the United States and Great Britain investigations have a customary basis, in France they have received statutory recognition, while in Germany, Austria, Belgium, and Poland provision is made for them in their respective constitutions.

The origin of investigations in England dates back to the middle of the 16th century. Investigations by Congress began only three years after the federal government was created. At the present time the number, frequency, and breadth of activity of congressional investigations far surpass that in any other country. In fact, only in the United States have investigations come to be regarded as instrumentalities of first-rate importance and of practically indispensable utility. We shall attempt to suggest the principal governmental factors which make this true. What features of the American system make investigations necessary? Why is it that in England, for example, the number of investigations is diminishing?

Before attempting to answer these queries two other introductory questions need to be considered. One is the definition of investigations. The other, to be considered first, is concerned with the nature of legislatures in modern democratic states. Especially, what are their functions? It is submitted that legislative investigations can be understood only as one bears in mind the fundamental nature and purpose of national legislatures in modern democracies.

The legislature is *dominium in dominio.* Only its general

rules of organization and powers are determined for it. Internally, it must make its own rules to preserve order. It must organize to assure the supremacy at all times of a party or coalition. In so far as the legislature does these things it tends to become efficient. The legislature, far more than either of the other departments of the government, operates in a broad field of discretion. With respect to its power to legislate it has unlimited discretion, except in those few cases in which constitutional provisions prohibit or limit this right. In the United States, for instance, where the powers of Congress are delegated to it by the Constitution, there is within these limits a plenary power to legislate. As a result there have grown up and been recognized by the courts an increasing number of powers which we call incidental powers. The right to make investigations is one of these.

The legislature, usually with the coöperation of a Ministry, determines the program of the government. Hence we call it the policy forming organ. In theory, of course, the legislature's action is carefully controlled by the will of the electorate. In reality its discretion is very wide. The legislature regulates the government by the laws it enacts. It sustains the other two branches, practically speaking, by the funds it appropriates. This latter control accounts for the legislature's superiority, in the absolute rather than legal sense, over the other two departments of the government. This statement must be modified when speaking of the United States. Here of course the only control which Congress exercises over the judicial branch is through impeachment proceedings. Even when the executive is tractable, the legislative body is invariably jealous of its traditional rival. Upon the slightest pretext it will encroach upon the executive domain.

The legislature gains further prestige and power by combining within its province executive and judicial aspects. As Professor Willoughby says concerning Congress: [1]

---

[1] W. W. Willoughby, Constitutional Law of the United States, I, 573.

In addition to their legislative powers the Houses of Congress have certain other powers, judicial or executive in character, such as, for example, with reference to impeachments, of punishing their members for disorderly conduct, or their expulsion if necessary, the determination of contested elections, etc. Each House of Congress has also, it has been held, the power to obtain information necessary for an intelligent exercise of its law-making power, and for this purpose to summon witnesses, and compel the production of documents, and to punish as contempt disobedience to orders thus given.

Legislatures, by means of customs, tend to fortify themselves strongly. True, they, like all the agencies of government, must change. But the legislative body invariably builds up a body of customary law. This feature is of great significance to our study, because investigations are a phase of this customary law. Within this " Lex et Consuetudo Parliamenti " the legislature moves, acts, and, so far as regards its internal structure at least, has its being. In this process the legislative body obeys the law of all organisms. It seeks to preserve itself.

Internal and External Responsibilities of Legislatures.— Generally speaking, we may say that the legislature has two chief responsibilities. To a large extent it is charged with the responsibility of organizing and regulating itself. It must put its own house in order and keep it so. In the second place, it must organize the judiciary and the executive. Further, even where there is the theory that the legislative and executive departments are independent, the legislature necessarily, to a large extent, must supervise and control the executive departments. The legislature is the regulator and censor of the executive domain, as well as the policy forming organ.

Now we are here concerned with both the internal and external problems of the deliberative assembly. Why? Simply because investigations may be and often are utilized in relation to the discharge of both the internal and external responsibilities of the legislature. Investigations help to fulfill the internal responsibility of the legislature. They may be utilized in judging the qualifications of members, or their behavior. Investigations are readily adapted to delving into any interferences or indignities which threaten the life of the assembly.

Externally, investigations may become very useful in helping the legislature's committees to obtain general information or specific facts needed for legislation. Again, investigations are one means of determining whether the law has been obeyed by the officers of the executive departments.

That the rôle of the legislative investigation often is as broad as stated is attested by the fact that in the chief constitutional governments of the present time investigations are actually utilized in all or some of the ways suggested. This results because no matter what differences may prevail in details, in general all legislatures have the same problems. Hence, the same general functions are evident in all of them. It is simple cause and effect, or problem and remedy. Where investigations are not utilized, some other device fulfilling the same need is found. We shall have occasion to consider this statement later in the chapter.

In General, Legislatures Have the Same Functions.—This conclusion need not be adopted without further argument. Let us consider briefly the chief functions of Parliament which have been pointed out by leading commentators upon the English Constitution, and then compare them to those of Congress. We shall not be able to carry the comparison farther than the United States. However, it may be said that the legislative assemblies of France and Germany, for instance, following more closely the English scheme of government than does the American, compare functionally with even greater precision than does Congress. Let us return to our original query. How completely do the actual functions of Congress correspond to the functions of the English Parliament? Perhaps we may well begin our consideration with the keen observer, Mr. Walter Bagehot.

Bagehot mentions five functions of Parliament.[2] First,

---

[2] Walter Bagehot, The English Constitution (1886), pp. 198-243.

there is the elective function. Parliament in effect elects and sustains a Ministry. Bagehot gives this function chief rank in importance. Next, there is the expressive function. Parliament interprets the mind of the English people. Third, Parliament possesses a teaching function. It alters society by instructing it. In the fourth place, there is the informing function. Parliament tells the people when things are well or when they are not. It watches the Crown and, if it errs, demands the redress of grievances and abuses. Finally, Parliament legislates. It makes laws for the realm. Contrary to the popular conception, Mr. Bagehot ranks this function last instead of first.

The classification of functions by Mr. Sidney Low,[3] written at a later date, is in some respects more satisfactory for a basis of comparison than Bagehot's. Low places legislation first. Then there is administration and executive control. In these respects he follows Bagehot. For the third function Low gives an independent status to the forming of financial policy and management of the public revenue. Bagehot considered this merely a phase of legislation. In the two remaining functions Mr. Low follows Bagehot. There is the discussion of abuses and the redress of grievances. The House of Commons is the ventilating chamber. Finally, Parliament tests and selects public men in debate, and elevates them to ministerial office.

The Rt. Hon. C. F. G. Masterman, writing at a still later date, points out only three parliamentary functions. These are the holding to accountability of the executive, the control of expenditures, and the making of laws.[4]

For reasons which soon will be explained, the writer prefers the last classification. But, assuming the more complex one of Mr. Bagehot for the moment, how does Congress measure up to the five functions which the noted English writer suggests? The comparison is most unfavorable with reference to the first function, the elective one. True, the Senate

[3] Sidney Low, The Governance of England (1913), pp. 59-154.
[4] Rt. Hon. C. F. G. Masterman, How England is Governed (1922), pp. 214-263.

cooperates in determining the personnel of the executive departments. Then, too, Congress repeatedly directs and controls administrative officers. It sometimes overrides their discretionary power. But, broadly speaking, Congress does not create the ministry. The cabinet plan and the presidential scheme are here most distinctly at variance.

However, in regard to the other four functions, the comparison is valid. Congress expresses the will of the people, and, conversely, instructs them. It holds government agents to accountability and discusses abuses. Finally, Congress makes laws.

But not everyone would agree that Congress does function in all these respects. We shall consider contentions to that effect shortly. Before doing that, though, let us consider the arguments for adopting the shorter classification of Mr. Masterman.

Shorter Classification of Functions Preferred.—Masterman's analysis appears preferable, for the purpose of the present study at least, because it is limited to only the essential functions of Parliament. Law-making, control of expenditure, and the censure and forcing from office of executive officials, are inescapable duties of the English and American legislature. But the legislature need not necessarily faithfully express the public will through law. It is not mandatory upon Parliament to teach the electorate. Of course it customarily does both of these things, but only incidentally to its three more inherent and necessary functions. As for creating the Ministry, Mr. Masterman prefers to consider the matter in relation to Parliament's control over it. Since Congress does not elect the executive we need not discuss the merits of Mr. Masterman's analysis in this respect.

The writer is convinced that the shorter analysis is preferable because. it readily permits of adding incidental functions to the list. For instance, there is every reason to assume that qualifying new members, preserving order, and safeguarding the legislative chamber and its members from interruption and attack are essentially as much functions of the legislature as informing public opinion.

Investigations May Aid the Fulfilment of Four Legislative Functions.—There is no reason to debate all the possible classifications of functions of legislatures which might be preferred.[5] Certain functions do undoubtedly exist. In our study of investigations we shall be concerned with four of them. Investigations aid law-making. They are readily available in pursuance of the function of qualifying, disciplining, and protecting members. This function we shall call the membership function. Finally, investigations are a powerful tool in assisting the legislature to hold the administrative and executive officers to accountability. Investigations may also be utilized to determine how funds have been spent. These two latter functions will be considered as one.

Investigations undoubtedly play an important part in informing the electorate. It is usually impossible to measure this influence. At any rate we shall not consider the moulding of public opinion except as an incidental result of investigations.

So much for a general consideration of the functions of legislatures. The question next arises, what are the attributes of investigations? What principal factors make them necessary?

Significance of Committees in the Legislative Process.—Mr. Bagehot says of the English Parliament that the dignified aspect of the House of Commons is altogether secondary to

---

[5] Undoubtedly one of the clearest and most thorough analyses of the functions of modern legislatures is that of Mr. W. F. Willoughby. He distinguishes seven legislative functions. The modern legislature acts as:

1. A constitutional assembly or constitutional convention;
2. A canvassing board and electoral college;
3. An organ of public opinion;
4. A board of directors for the government corporation;
5. An organ of legislation;
6. An executive council;
7. A high court of justice.

(W. F. Willoughby, The Government of Modern States, 290, 291.)

its efficient use. This consideration is even more true of the American Congress. We often hear Congress spoken of as if its chief characteristic were that the two chambers deliberate. As a matter of fact they rarely do anything of the sort. What does actually happen is that most of the work of Congress is done in committees and in party caucuses. There it is that facts and policies are thrashed out. The committee particularly is the efficient factor of the legislative process. The debate or deliberation which is supposed to take place in the respective halls of Congress is for the most part party banter and propaganda for consumption by the folks at home.

Investigating Committees Obtain Facts Difficult to Access.—If the legislature is to learn the facts of legislative proposals it must rely chiefly upon its committees. These committees, in turn, must know the facts of a situation before they can act efficiently. Of course the facts are not brought to light in many cases. This may result from a desire that they should not be divulged, or from the difficulty of obtaining them. The primary purpose of investigation is to obtain the facts of a difficult situation. It is only natural that a committee should be chosen for this work. It is the efficient way. Likewise, it has been found that when it comes to considering and acting upon revealed facts, the standing committee can do this with more dispatch and competence than the whole body of members.

Factors Complicating the Fact-finding Process.—It is hardly disputable that the problem of obtaining information for legislative functions is more complicated in the United States than in any other constitutional government of the present time. The first factor which makes it difficult to know the facts of a situation is the very size of the nation. It is absurd to suppose that a relatively small group of citizens, in Congress assembled, will know at first hand sufficient facts to enable it to legislate wisely upon affairs so complicated as, for example, Muscle Shoals or Boulder Dam, and the drainage problem of the Mississippi. A second factor, of equal significance, is the diversity of interests in the country, growing out of its sectionalism. In the third place, there is the separation of the legislative and executive departments. Yet Congress must learn somehow whether the officers of the government are conducting themselves and are expending funds allotted to them according to the law and intent of Congress.

Finally, there is the so-called big business problem. The government has launched out upon a policy of extensive social and economic control. The situation in all its phases is by no means mastered. Further regulation and control demands more knowledge of existing conditions. Moreover, as an incident to the fulfillment of their internal responsibility, the houses of Congress must often obtain information concerning their own members.

The first attribute of congressional investigations therefore is their uniform aim of obtaining information. Of course it is recognized that in acting upon any proposal of legislation the ordinary standing committees obtain information. They may, and often do, make an informal investigation, at times even holding public hearings. But we must distinguish between such informal investigations and formal investigations. We have drawn one distinction already, namely, that formal investigations are generally concerned with difficult subject-matter. The theory is that they shall get information which is not regularly or readily obtained. The second characteristic of formal investigations is the fact that their activity is inquisitorial.

Congress Cannot Always Rely Upon Casual Information.— There are many casual ways in which Congress may and actually does obtain knowledge. There are the demands of the local constituents. Group interests in and outside of Washington carry on a constant campaign with the purpose of making Congressmen think and vote as the interests desire. Then, too, the newspapers are undoubtedly the greatest informative force in the country. Other minor factors could be mentioned.

2

Two criticisms apply to the possibility of considering these casual sources of information as sufficient. To begin with, their motive in informing Congress is to a very large extent determined by partisan, sectional, social, fraternal, industrial, or religious interests. The good of the nation is concerned only indirectly. The prime motive power is selfish. Therefore the proposals of these groups are often unreliable and inadequate.

What Congress must learn is not what certain persons or groups choose to say about a situation, but what is actually the case when all interested and non-motivated witnesses have been forced to reveal what they have not told or felt disposed to tell. This feature of investigations cannot be too forcefully stressed. That a principal aspect of investigations is their inquisitorial nature is proved by the fact that investigating committees, with very few exceptions, are armed with power to demand the testimony of witnesses, and the production of necessary papers and documents. Failure to comply with such demands is punished by severe penalties.

Committee of Investigation Defined.—A committee of investigation is a select or standing committee of the legislature. It is created by a resolution of the commissioning chamber. The purpose of the projected investigation is described with considerable detail in a resolution or resolutions. The committee's rights and duties are thus circumscribed. The principal aim is simply to investigate and report, not to frame legislation. The chamber itself rarely acts directly upon the report of the investigating committee. The report is adopted and referred to one of the standing committees. The power of obtaining evidence by summoning witnesses or demanding papers may be exercised only when specifically granted in the resolution, or if later bestowed. In short, the investigating committee is a fact-finding auxiliary of the commissioning house. The chamber creates it, clothes it with power, sets limits to its activity, and finally terminates its existence. The demise of the investigating committee usually comes with the end of the chamber's sessional life.

Confusion of Thought Concerning the Nature and Functions of Congress.—Our next inquiry shall be directed to the question of whether or not Congress, a legislature of enumerated powers, does possess the functions of controlling expenditures and of supervising the administration. As suggested above, it is sometimes denied that Congress possesses these powers. Some, who discover in the intent of the framers and the words of the Constitution a closely defined and utterly inescapable separation of powers, contend that the sole and only legitimate function of Congress is to legislate—to make "genuine laws." [6] The antithesis of this position is represented in the statement of Dr. Lindsay Rogers, who contends that "legislatures in modern constitutional governments . . . have a three-fold purpose: they legislate, they control expenditure, and they supervise the administration." [7] In reviewing the book just quoted Representative Luce unequivocally challenges this assertion, and asks: "Where is there any proof that, at any rate in the United States, a legislature has any business to interfere with the spending of money that has been appropriated, or to supervise the administration of law?" [8] He then suggests that these may be natural functions under ministerial responsibility, but that there is no warrant for them in American constitutions, state or federal.

It appears that Mr. Luce is convinced that ours is a constitution of completely separated powers, and that it can prosper only as we adhere with strictness to a system according to which Congress makes the laws, sublimely heedless of whether former laws have been or are being carried out, or whether funds once appropriated are being legally spent or are being pocketed by officials. Apparently it is not of much persuasive value to Mr. Luce that Congress is actually functioning in all three ways suggested by Dr. Rogers. Congress ought not to do these things even if both Houses have exercised all three powers from the beginning. The idea that

---

[6] Robert Luce, Congress (Harvard University Press 1926).
[7] Lindsay Rogers, The American Senate, 192. (New York 1926).
[8] The American Political Science Review, XXI, No. 1, 179.

Congress is simply a law-making body cannot be seriously entertained.

Three Chief Functions of Congress Must Be Recognized.— The writer adheres to the position taken by Dr. Lindsay Rogers, inasmuch as the written Constitution has no meaning without interpretation, and moreover Congress, in working out the relation between the three departments has, by long practice, come to legislate, to control expenditures, and to supervise the administration. The writer sees in the steady increase of the range and minuteness of Congress' regulation of personnel and expenditure matters an appreciable gain in governmental efficiency and a harbinger of administrative responsibility tantamount to that in parliamentary countries. The reasons for Mr. Luce's entertaining an opposite point of view may be found in his theory of responsibility.[9]

Law-making is one of Congress' purposes, as it is but one of Parliament's. Equally as important are Congress' duties of controlling the finances and of supervising the administration. A long continued practice of exercising investigative powers in pursuance of the two latter functions adds additional evidence of their acceptability upon a plane of equality with the law-making function.

---

[9] Speaking of just this matter of responsibility, he says: " Another argument is that the executive should be responsible for carrying out every detail. In this matter of ' responsibility ' great confusion prevails. Responsibility implies punishment. What could be more unjust than to require responsibility of president or governor for the whole operation of government, to deal out to him punishment for every incapacity, every inefficiency, every failure? American common sense never has accepted, never will accept, any such idea. We do not choose with it in mind. A political party may be put into office in the hope that it will better administer affairs, or be turned out because it has badly administered them, but the question is always one of totals, not of details. Only in the rarest instances do we punish any executive because of the shortcomings of minor officials. Broad policies may and should determine the fate of the President, but his political fortunes ought not to depend on the work of individual administrative agents " (Luce, op cit., 71). "Responsibility" does not connote "punishment," to the writer, but rather the idea of amenability to the supervision and control of a directing agency, the policy-forming organ, which is Congress.

The Functions of Congressional Investigations.—The scope of the investigative power encompasses more than the three legislative purposes mentioned by Dr. Rogers. It has been stated that Congress possesses primarily law-making, finance-controlling, and administration-supervising functions.[10] In addition there is the constitutional privilege accorded each House of Congress of judging the qualifications and behavior of its members. These stipulations, and another concerning the protection to members for any words spoken in debate, have made necessary another group of investigations. These constitutional powers of Congress will be called Congress' membership function.

Hence, for separate treatment in succeeding chapters we shall consider the three functions of congressional committees of investigation to be: (1) Inquiry with reference to members, (2) Investigation in pursuance of the law-making function, and (3) Inquiry as an instrumentality to control the executive division in carrying out the legislative will.

Position of the Administration in the Government.—The constitutionality of investigations concerning members of Congress cannot be the subject of serious judicial questioning.[11] Likewise with respect to inquiries in aid of the law-making function, the Supreme Court has held the authority necessary and proper as an implied power.[12] It is only with regard to the question of investigations regarding the execu-

---

[10] For the purpose of discussing examples of the different kinds of investigations it has been deemed advisable to consider the finance-controlling and the administration-supervising functions of Congress under a single heading. As a matter of fact, the two functions are not easily distinguishable. When Congress launches an investigation of some phase of the administrative service it is well-nigh impossible to differentiate between Congress' concern with reference to the misapplication of funds and its concern with regard to the misconduct of its servant who was responsible for such abuse. However, when in authorizing an investigation Congress makes it clearly appear that the purpose is predominantly either financial or administrative, the distinction will be observed in our consideration. For purposes of legal treatment the power will be considered unitary.

[11] Below, Chaps. iii, vi.

[12] Below, Chaps. iv, vi.

tion of Congress' policy that one finds an unsatisfactory recognition of the equal validity of the power. In order to appreciate the significance of the problem in considering investigations of the executive, and in order later to appraise the legality of the power, we shall consider the position of the Administration in the government.

Here at once one recognizes the desirability of responsible cabinet government. Under such a system the position of the administration is fixed and sure. No doubt arises as to whether it shall be controlled by the legislature or by the Cabinet. The contrary, however, has from the very beginning been true in the United States. As a matter of fact, the trouble arises because the Framers of the Constitution did not think of the Administration as a distinct branch of the government, and hence made no provision for it.[13]

Technically, as well as in practice, the difference which exists between the administrative and executive offices is generally recognized. The executive department of the government is understood to be the politically actuated, ordinance-making, program initiating, division of the government. The Constitution charges it with seeing that the laws are faithfully executed. Policy forming rests mostly in the legislative branch, but it is also shared to some extent by those executive officials who have discretionary powers not subject to court control.

On the other hand, the Administration executes the details of general policy and the minutiae of the law. It is responsible to the one who determines policy or makes the law. Its competency is largely, indeed almost exclusively, non-discretionary. Congress, which created the departments, is faced with the necessity of constantly regulating them, and therefore needs to learn of the details of their conduct.

---

[13] The author has drawn heavily upon the published treatises of Mr. W. F. Willoughby, Director of the Institute of Government Research, in considering this subject. Acknowledgment is due to Mr. Willoughby especially for his having put at the writer's disposal a manuscript, at that time unpublished, on " Principles of Public Administration." In reference to this matter the reader is also advised to refer to Frank J. Goodnow, Politics and Administration.

Besides the indefiniteness which is bound to exist because no unequivocal provision was made for the control of the administration,[14] the problem is complicated by an attempt to solve the problem by a strict application of the separation of powers doctrine. Literal constructionists reason that the administration must belong either wholly to the President or to Congress. Such a position is not logically necessary or practically possible.

The President and the various cabinet officers may be thought of as exercising routine control; but Congress, being the creator, sustainer, and policy forming organ for the departments, must be conceded the final determination in disciplining the personnel or remoulding the duties of the administrative services. This necessitates the right of making investigations.

When one considers certain features of the adjustment as it has been worked out so far there is an inclination to decide that the President is the sole and rightful head of the administration. Does not the President actually exercise a large number of administrative functions? No one can doubt, for example, that in creating the State and War departments Congress vested very large powers of personal supervision and control in the President. Is it not also true that the Myers decision, by giving the President the power of removal without the consent of the Senate, of executory officers appointed by him with such consent, more firmly fixed the right of the President to be the actual head of the administration?[15]

---

[14] Mr. Willoughby does not overstate the case when he says: "The fact of the matter is that our government represents one in which, neither the theory of the union of powers, nor that of a separation of powers, has been consistently carried out. In framing our Constitution its authors proceeded upon the theory that all the powers of government were divisible into the three great branches of legislative, judicial, and executive and that separate provision should be made for each. They failed utterly to recognize or to make any direct provision for the exercise of administrative powers. In consequence of this failure our entire constitutional history has been marked by a struggle between the legislative and executive branches as to the relative parts that they should play in the exercise of this power "(The Government of Modern States, 242).

[15] Frank S. Meyers vs. United States, 272 U. S. 52.

The first reply to be made is that the framers of the Constitution undoubtedly had no further expectation than that the President should be only the political head. As Dr. W. W. Willoughby states:

It was undoubtedly intended that the President should be little more than a political chief; that is to say, one whose function should in the main consist in the performance of those political duties which are not subject to judicial control. It was quite clear that it was intended that he should not, except to those political matters, be the administrative head of the government with general powers of directing and controlling the acts of subordinate federal administrative agents.[16]

Congress as a Board of Directors.—The legal and political relationship between the executive and legislative departments has been clarified by Mr. W. F. Willoughby. He terms the former the " General Manager," and the latter the " Board of Directors " of the government's business.[17] Congress determines the general policy and is the tribunal of last resort in questions of whether or not its will is being executed faithfully by the Administration.

" This constitutional power of Congress to keep the reins of final administrative control in its own hands rather than in those of the President," states Mr. Willoughby, " has been amply sustained by the courts."[18] In the case of Kendall vs. United States [19] the Supreme Court, in affirming the decision of the circuit court, said:

The executive power is vested in a President, and as far as his powers are derived from the Constitution, he is beyond the reach of any other department, except in the mode prescribed by the Constitution through the impeaching power. But it by no means follows that every officer in every branch of that department is under the exclusive direction of the President. Such a principle, we apprehend, is not, certainly cannot, be claimed by the President. There are certain political duties imposed upon many officers in the executive departments, the discharge of which is under the direction of the President. But it would be an alarming doctrine that Congress cannot impose

---

[16] The Constitutional Law of the United States, 1156. Cf. Goodnow, Principles of American Administrative Law, 78.
[17] W. F. Willoughby, Principles of Public Administration, 9-34.
[18] Ibid., see the early case of Kendall vs. United States, 5 Cranch, C. C. 163.
[19] 12 Peters, 524.

upon any executive officer any duty they may think proper, which is not repugnant to any rights secured and protected by the Constitution, and in such cases, the duty and responsibility grow out of and are subject to the control of the law and not to the direction of the President. And this is emphatically the case where the duty enjoined is of a mere ministerial character.

Mr. Willoughby concludes his examination of this subject by saying, " The constitutional doctrine thus early declared as to the relation of the Congress to the administrative services which it establishes, and of those services to the President, has not since been disturbed and fixes today the legal status of the executive departments." [20]

Congress, as a board of directors, has several functions to fulfill. One of the most important is that of supervision and control. However, Mr. Willoughby shows that this responsibility is only the natural outgrowth of six correlated functions. These duties of Congress as a board of directors he summarizes as follows: (1) Determination of activities to be undertaken; (2) determination of agencies and organization to be employed in performing such activities; (3) determination of the personnel of such agencies; (4) determination of the rules of procedure to be employed by such agencies; (5) determination of the amount of funds that shall be rendered available for the performance of such activities and the maintenance of such agencies; (6) determination of the means that shall be provided for supervising and controlling these agencies to the end that assurance may be had that they are faithfully and efficiently carrying out all orders given to them. Investigations, it will be observed, are one of the means for carrying out the last named duty.

Congressional Methods of Obtaining Information.—In his book, " Congress," Representative Luce points out that, " Probably more than half the business, measured by impor-

---

[20] W. F. Willoughby, op. cit. Says Mr. Willoughby elsewhere: " In a very true sense all the administrative officers of the government, including the President himself, when the performance of administrative duties has been entrusted to him, are but agents of Congress and subject to its orders and control " (The Government of Modern States, 253).

tance, comes directly or indirectly from the departments or bureaus of the government." [21]   Congress, sitting as a board of directors, must obtain a great deal of information about the departments before it can legislate or vote appropriations. This necessitates constant supervision and control.

Mr. Willoughby says:

A study of the problem shows that the means through which this supervision and control may be exercised and accountability enforced are the following: (1) The requirement that all administrative officers shall keep proper records of their official acts; (2) the requirement that these officers shall at stated intervals, and at least once a year, submit reports giving a full account of their acts; (3) the requirement that accurate accounts shall be kept of all financial transactions and reports of such transactions be made in such form that full information regarding their character is furnished; (4) provision for a system of examination or audit of these accounts with a view to determining their accuracy and legality; (5) provision for the consideration by the legislative bodies, acting directly or through properly constituted committees, of the administrative and financial reports with a view to determining not merely the legality of the action taken, but also the efficiency and economy with which official duties have been performed; (6) the requirement that administrative officers shall furnish information regarding specific acts by them when called upon so to do by the legislative bodies; and (7) provision for special investigations or inquiries of a comprehensive character of the manner in which affairs have been conducted by a particular service or services.[22]

Investigations as a Measure of Last Resort.—The important point to be observed in the above analysis is that congressional investigations are a last resort among the methods of obtaining information. In other words, the number and importance of investigations of this nature are in proportion to the deficiencies in the permanent apparatus for obtaining information and exercising control. Were the established, that is to say permanent, controls satisfactory, investigations as a final extreme measure would not be necessary.

Nowhere is this more clearly manifest than in the financial experience of the United States. President Taft stated upon good authority in his message to Congress of June 27, 1912, that of over one hundred investigations conducted by com-

---

[21] Robert Luce, Congress, 3-4.
[22] W. F. Willoughby, Principles of Public Administration, 30.

mittees of Congress since 1810, a majority of them were for the purpose of determining the expenditure of public funds. The evil, he said, grew out of an inadequate and inefficient system of budget and accounting procedure. The adoption of the Good Budget Bill in 1921,[23] based upon the plan President Taft had advocated, brought a degree of efficiency into the fiscal organization which it is still too early to appreciate fully.[24]

The Court Has Not Recognized the Validity of Investigations Designed to Uncover Misconduct of Officials.—It is an unfortunate fact that the Supreme Court of the United States has never flatly recognized the fitness and propriety of the investigative process in relation to Congress' supervisory power over the administration. When opportunity was apparently provided for such an avowal in the case of McGrain *vs.* Daugherty,[25] the court satisfied itself by declaring the investigation of the Attorney General necessary and proper on the ground that such information was needed for the " efficient exercise of the legislative function." By this indefinite phrase " the legislative function," the Court apparently meant the law-making function.

---

[23] Below, Chap. vii.

[24] The condition which existed previous to this is graphically described by Mr. W. F. Willoughby as follows: " Prior to the creation of this office (the Comptroller-General) the only means that Congress had of controlling the administration with a view to satisfying itself that its orders were being honestly and efficiently carried out was by calling for information through the passage of resolutions of inquiry and through special investigations made from time to time by its regular or special committees. These means were thoroughly inadequate, unsatisfactory, and expensive, due in large part to the fact that the investigations thus made were occasional and spasmodic. They were frequently of a partisan character and those making them lacked a staff technically competent to bring out and interpret the facts. That the ten committees on expenditure of the departments of the House failed to perform any important service as a means of control over the administration, is well known. It should furthermore be borne in mind that our political system makes no provision for the device of interpellations, which in states having a responsible form of government is an effective means of inquiring into the conduct of administrative officers " (W. F. Willoughby, The National Budget System, 21).

[25] 273 U. S. 135, 71 L. ed. 370. This case is considered fully, below, Chap. vi.

The Federal District Court of Ohio, in the original decision of the case and upon the same statement of facts, held the exercise of the power illegal because it was judicial in its nature.[26] Neither court, in the writer's opinion, recognized the actual nature and purpose of such investigations.

Investigations of the executive departments are necessary and proper not only because the Houses of Congress must learn the needs of the departments in legislating, but because they do possess and have consistently exercised from the first the power to see that the departments are conducted in accordance with law and policy. When Congress suspects, for good and sufficient reason, that irregularities are taking place in a department, it is its duty and privilege under the Constitution to investigate as a means to "other action." The fact that Congress might, and probably was considering "other action" [27] in the Daugherty case (such as divulging sufficient evidence for civil or criminal prosecution in the courts) should be no bar to the investigation's legality.

Investigations of the executive in England prior to 1776 were matters of common knowledge to the framers of the Constitution. While some of the framers were in early Congresses, investigations of this nature were authorized. The power has been exercised increasingly ever since. In the Daugherty case the court placed great emphasis upon the early exercise and continued practice of the investigative powers. They say:

We are of opinion that the power of inquiry—with process to enforce it—is an essential and appropriate auxiliary to the legislative function. It was so regarded and employed in American legislatures before the Constitution was framed and ratified. Both Houses of Congress took this view of it early in their history—the House of Representatives with the approving vote of Mr. Madison and other members whose service in the convention which framed the Constitution gives special significance to their action . . . and both houses have employed the power accordingly up to the present

---

[26] 299 Fed. 620.
[27] The resolution in the Daugherty case stated that "other action" was being contemplated. The Supreme Court held this meaningless, since not within Congress' competence (273 U. S. 138).

time. . . . A long-continued practical construction by Congress of powers under provisions of the Constitution should be taken as fixing the meaning of such provisions.[28]

A careful consideration of examples of the early and long-continued practice of making investigations respecting the conduct of executive officials should convince one that there is no adequate reason for the court's not recognizing the propriety of the power of supervision and control, on a plane of equality with the other two functions of Congress.[29]

Inauguration of Investigations in the United States.— The author has hoped to show from the foregoing that, contrary to the assertions of those who would limit the province of Congress to mere law-making, it actually possesses and has exercised from the beginning the three functions recognized in legislatures possessing plenary powers of legislation. Congress, as the board of directors of the government, finds it difficult to obtain information from and to keep control over the administrative services. The situation is not at all satisfactory. In governments of the responsible type such a situation does not arise. This factor is the chief difference accounting for the greater number and importance of investigations in the United States. But we are anticipating. Such a comparative analysis is what we proposed to consider as the second problem of this chapter.

One point, however, remains before taking up the comparative phases of the study. It appears apropos and equally important to show why it is possible for minorities in Congress to force resolutions of investigation to be adopted. This is unquestionably a factor accounting in considerable measure for the greater number of investigations in the United States as compared with European governments of the responsible type.

If the inquisitorial power exercised by Congress were as inoffensive as it is considered in theory, namely, if its only purpose were merely to determine a question of fact necessary

---

[28] Ibid.   [29] Below, Chap. v.

in legislating, one would not expect the party equation to be an important factor in the genesis of investigations. The average layman, however, knows that the keynote of many investigations is a crusading zeal to expose the inefficiency and corruption of the majority party. The fact is that the power of investigation is not a matter of right, but a question of privilege—a privilege which oftentimes must be bartered for, or if need be, coerced.

The proof of this point is demonstrated in the varying difficulty with which investigations may be instituted in the House and in the Senate, respectively. The interesting thing is that comparing the present time with the early days of Congress the tables have completely turned. We shall see in a later chapter that in the first forty years after the Constitution had been adopted the House conducted seven or eight times as many investigations as did the Senate. Furthermore, not until 1818 did the Senate institute an inquiry of any importance, or give a committee the right to send for persons and papers.[30]

Dr. Rogers tells the other side of the story, namely, that of the greater activity by the Senate in recent times. In fact, at the present time one should speak of "Senatorial" investigations because the House is apparently relinquishing its activity in this regard, while the Senate is increasing its concern.[31] The indisputable cause of this transformation is found in the fact that partly through necessity and partly through preference the House has gradually made sufferance of minority interference impossible,[32] while the Senate still may be the scene of "unrestricted garrulity," even of successful filibusters.

---

[30] Below, Chap. iii.

[31] Lindsay Rogers, The American Senate, 161-190.

[32] By far the most significant proof of the impotance of a House minority to launch an investigation is provided in the proposed investigation of Secretary Daugherty. The investigation was vigorously demanded by a large number of proponents. The resolution was pocketed by the Rules Committee and attempts to gain its discharge were fruitless (P. D. Hasbrouck, Party Government in the House of Representatives, 113, 114, 115, 149, 150).

Further examination shows undeniably that an adequate comprehension of the manner in which investigations originate may be had only by recognizing the close relationship of closure and of parliamentary rules generally to the passage of resolutions of inquiry. Dr. Rogers is responsible for pointing out that " the importance of rules can hardly be overestimated. Once a matter of convenience, and designed to secure order in an assembly where contradictory aspirations struggle with each other, they are now frequently weapons of personal and party warfare. They may have as much influence as the Constitution itself on the conduct of public business." [33] The fact is that rules for limiting debate have become so effective in the House, where majority control is complete, that in late years the House has not conducted as many or as important investigations as the Senate.[34] With the exception of the Graham committee which scrutinized military expenditures during the war, practically every important investigation of the last three Congresses has been carried on by Senate committees.

The reason for this is that the Senate is such a forum that a resolution of inquiry favored by a minority has good prospects of success. Since debate is not limited, the need for investigations can be brought out. Closure cannot easily be invoked. Were the party steam roller set into motion to defeat the resolution the minority could effectively answer in the form of a filibuster which would endanger the majority's timetable. Each party feels that its success depends in large part upon carrying to completion by the end of the congressional session the constructive program of legislation which the party has outlined. Rather than be thwarted in this, it is usually the case that administration leaders are willing to allow a motion for an investigation to be approved by the Rules Committee in order to avoid the possibility of the alternative, namely, the filibuster. This is especially true as the Senate approaches the end of the session. Thus it is that

---

[33] Rogers, The American Senate, 119-20.
[34] Ibid., pp. 201-204.

investigations of significant public importance, especially those relating to the finances and the executive departments, derive their right to be from the whip handle which the minority holds, the filibuster.

To be sure, it is a different matter when the President and the majority of either or both houses are of different political faiths. Then investigations are not only possible, but they incline to be numerous. For instance, during President Wilson's last two years, there were fifty-one congressional investigations in progress or being proposed at one time. But with a normal alignment it is practically impossible to get a resolution for inquiry past the several lines of defense in the House, and in the Senate the majority leaders are no more anxious to act of their own accord, especially when through party fortune their own careers are at stake.

Therefore, when persons speak of the " right " of a legislative majority to transact its business without dilatory opposition, one is forced to conclude that they have not considered the essential nature of the problem involved. We have said that ours is certainly not a responsible cabinet form of government, and that many analogies are not applicable. Filibusters are the only restraint upon majority despotism. Closure blocks the road to accountability in high places. Filibusters are essential to major public investigations.

Investigations May Be Largely Supplanted by Other Agencies.—Granted, that if investigations are really necessary and desirable, the closure rules of the legislature should not be so strict as to preclude the reasonable certainty of setting investigations afoot. But, after all, are investigations inevitable? Why not alter the permanent machinery in order to meet more satisfactorily the functions now fulfilled by investigations? We shall attempt to answer but the first of these two questions in this chapter. In other words, it will be our purpose to show that other governments, although faced by the same problems which make investigations necessary in the United States, have worked out other more permanent means of fulfilling these functions.

Committees of inquiry, viewed historically, have played a salutary rôle in representative government. But this exposes only one-half of the complete picture. It cannot be said too forcibly that most investigations, no matter in what government they are conducted, represent only a sporadic effort upon the part of the legislature to achieve ends which could and should be attained through permanently established agencies in the normal governmental structure. Investigations are usually a weapon of last resort. They are the unusual in the regular routine of government. Their use is justified only when the government is so organized, or under-organized, that necessary functions of the government would not be efficiently cared for otherwise.

How the Necessity for Investigations in Pursuance of the Membership Function Has Been Obviated in England.—The total number of investigations by English Parliamentary committees is steadily declining. Professor Redlich points out that between 1878 and 1913, their frequency was cut almost in half.[35] Our problem is to discover, if possible, the chief factors accounting for this.

As we shall learn in the next chapter, investigations in pursuance of Parliament's membership function have probably been the most numerous of all classes of investigation. This was true at least until recent years. It will also be shown that inquiries of this nature have been and still are numerous in the United States. England has now worked out a means of deciding election disputes which is more strictly judicial in nature, and more satisfactory in its results than the doubtful recourse to investigation.

The chief criticism of deciding electoral disputes by means of investigating committees is that the judicial process is involved in such cases, and investigating committees, ruled by party considerations, cannot as a rule be expected to decide in a judicial manner. Then, too, there is nothing to prevent the district whose representative is being investigated from

---

[35] Joseph Redlich, Procedure of the House of Commons, II, 187.

3

being obliged to remain without full representation for an
extended period, due to the delay of the investigating committee.

Mr. Cecil S. Emden attests that a situation similar to that
described by the writer long prevailed in England. After
pointing out that the Commons successfully asserted the
right to decide their cases of disputed elections in the six-
teenth century, he says: " The position was a difficult one.
The Commons were impelled to retain the jurisdiction, as
concerning their own constitution; and yet it was apparent
that every disputed case would, owing to the inherent frailty
of politicians, be treated as one to test the strength of political parties." [36]

The system of judicial determination which has replaced
the need of investigating committees, may be thought of as a
compromise. Now the trial of disputed election cases is
entrusted to two judges of the King's Bench Division of the
High Court.[37] These judges are so appointed that the Legislature or the Executive is not in a position to influence their
judgment. When the judges have reached their decision they
certify it to the Speaker. But the decision and the action to
be taken upon it are matters for the legislature, by right, if
not by common practice. After the judgment has been certi-
fied, it is accordingly entered upon the Journals of the House
and the necessary directions are given by the House for carrying the decision into execution. Therefore the system really
amounts to the House of Commons' retaining the form of
jurisdiction, while the substance of it is in the Judiciary.

We shall advert to this plan in a later chapter on the membership function in the United States. It has been cited here
to show that investigations may be replaced by permanent

---

[36] Cecil S. Emden, Principles of British Constitutional Law
(1925), 52, 53.

[37] If the matter in dispute relates to the legal qualifications of
the elected candidate, and not to the manner of his election, it is
investigated by the House itself and is not referred to the judges
of the High Court for recommendation (Munro, Governments of
Europe, 154, 155).

devices, even in the case of a function like the electoral one, in which the legislature's constitution is so intimately involved.

Royal Commissions in England as Auxiliaries to Parliament's Law-making Function.—No one would deny that law-making, by the nature of the process, requires information of a very comprehensive and often technical quality. If the inquisitorial power is justified anywhere in the government, its use is certainly most appropriate in pursuance of the law-making function. But again the query arises, are investigating committees necessary to the efficient exercise of the law-making function, or can this function be better fulfilled through permanently established channels?

Both in England and in the United States investigating committees have, from the first, investigated problems of a complicated nature, or disturbances of the public peace, in order to aid the whole body of law-makers. In England at the present time such investigations are very rare. Authorities tell us that one of the chief reasons for the steady decrease in the number and importance of investigations of this general nature is the increasing reliance of Parliament upon Royal Commissions. These commissions are controlled by the executive division, and have authority to pursue their investigations longer than the session of one Parliament.[38]

An interesting instance of the sort of thing done by commissions of this kind is found in the inquiry and report of the Royal Commission on London Government. In 1911 the London County Council, chafing under limitations imposed upon it by Parliament, invited a careful inquiry into the whole question of London Government with a view to a possible extension of the county's boundaries and a corresponding increase in the council's power. The commission consti-

---

[38] Professor Redlich states: "Almost all the great reforms of the nineteenth century in internal administration, taxation, education, labour protection, and other social questions, have been based on the full investigations made by royal commissions. . . ." (Redlich, Procedure of the House of Commons, II, 193).

tuted by Parliament, however, after considering claims and counter-claims, decided that enhancement of the council's powers was not advisable. Under the broad commission granted by Parliament they recommended that there should be a reapportionment of existing functions between the council and the metropolitan borough councils.[39]

Royal Commissions have been found to possess several factors of superiority over investigating committees. First, their tenure being longer, they are in a position to delve more exhaustively into the matter at hand. Again, the commission is less apt to be constituted from political bias because it permits the inclusion in its personnel of experts and scientific men. Finally, they are the means of rendering the law-making process more efficient, because by often employing non-members of Parliament, they obviate the costly inroads upon the time of members ordinarily accompanying membership upon an investigating committee.

Exception should be made in favor of the advisability of investigating committees when the public safety is involved. It cannot be gainsaid that public exigencies demand rapid and readily available means of investigation. Disturbing public occurrences can be handled competently by Parliamentary committees of inquiry. This fact has apparently been recognized. Professor Redlich is authority for the statement in 1908 that, " At the present time, this [investigations of public occurrences] is the main function of select committees if we leave out of consideration those upon private bills." [40]

Factors in England and France Eliminating the Necessity for Investigations of the Administration.—England and France are several steps ahead of the United States in the establishment by their legislatures of permanent devices for fulfilling the function of control over the services of the government. Chief among these agencies are Cabinet responsi-

---

[39] Report of the Royal Commission on London Government (London 1923).

[40] Redlich, op. cit., II, 206.

bility, "grievance before supply," well established systems of financial budgeting and comptrolling, the Parliamentary "question," and, peculiar to France, the system of interpellations. It is not contended, of course, that all of these factors are of equal importance or that there are not objectionable features in some of them.

Nevertheless these devices do prove that investigations are not inevitable in fulfilling the supervision and control function. The most important object lesson derived from a consideration of these comparative factors is that when direct responsibility in money and administrative matters increases, the need for investigations decreases.

Where there is responsibility for ministerial acts the legislature is not faced with the necessity of attempting to obtain compliance with its laws and regulations by investigations, which at the best can enforce only the letter and not the spirit of its mandates. The primary reason accounting for efficiency in the administration, and consequently calling for a negligible number of investigations, is set forth lucidly by Mr. Bagehot. "The efficient secret of the English Constitution," says he, "may be described as the close union, the nearly complete fusion, of the executive and legislative powers. No doubt by the traditional theory, as it exists in all the books, the goodness of our Constitution consists in the entire separation of the legislative and executive authorities, but in truth its merit consists in their singular approximation." [41]

It appears that leading members of President Harding's cabinet were not even asked for an opinion concerning the Naval Oil leases, and it is doubtful if the matter was discussed. It is impossible to imagine such an irresponsible proceeding upon an important question in a cabinet government, where the serious blunder of one Cabinet official is likely to cause the overthrow of the entire Cabinet.

No more efficient method of obtaining responsibility and

---

[41] Bagehot, op. cit., 78, 79.

therewith the lessening of the number of investigations could probably be found than the traditional English method of "grievance before supply." Other features of this system, such as the question and the counter-question, we shall consider later. Our concern now is with the financial arrangement of England, for after all, more depends upon that feature in any government than upon any other. When the government is asking Parliament to provide the money for carrying on the work of any department, the House of Commons, first through a committee, and second when the decision of its committee is reported to the House, has opportunities given to attack any suspected delinquencies in that department.

The common procedure is to propose the reduction in salary of the Minister responsible for the alleged shortcoming. Under such a proposal the action of anyone in the department attacked may be questioned, because the Minister is responsible for all. If the motion of censure is carried, the unforunate Minister does not lose the proposed reduction of salary. As Masterman puts it,[42] "He loses all his salary, and his colleagues also. For, unless they attempt to reverse what they may interpret as a snap vote, unrepresentative of the real opinion of the House, they must resign. And in any case a succession of such snap votes would ensure their resignation."

We cannot complete this survey of the relationship of governmental organization to the problem of obviating investigations without some mention of the dominant control exerted by the English financial system.[43] Recent developments in the United States have made the two systems similar in broad outline. Still, in England there is greater responsibility in expenditures, and a happier adjustment in the preparation and expenditure of appropriations by the same authority.

---

[42] Masterman, How England is Governed, 226.
[43] The best treatment of this subject is found in "The System of Financial Administration of Great Britain," prepared by Messrs. W. F. Willoughby, W. W. Willoughby, and S. M. Lindsay, for the Institute of Government Research (New York, 1917).

This authority is vested in the Cabinet and is exercised by the real practical administrator, the Chancellor of the Exchequer. So complete is the control of the Comptroller and Auditor-General that practically nothing can be done in any of the departments in the way of changing the details of expenditure, the salaries of clerks, the allocation of funds, or even the duties of employees, without the approval of the Treasury.

Even more than in the United States, the function of the Comptroller is to investigate and report.[44] He has no authority to discipline, as this is left to the Chancellor of the Exchequer or in the last resort to the Cabinet. So well established is this procedure by long custom that there is not the resentment and friction in the departments one finds at present in the United States.

Of equal importance to responsible financial control in checking the demand for investigations, is the rôle played by questions addressed to Ministers. There can be little doubt that investigations usually arise out of the suspicions of a minority not in power, and nothing is so potent with inquisitorial probabilities as the vague murmurings and uninformed opinions of such a group. For that reason, therefore, the English " question " is undoubtedly one of the largest contributing factors toward checking demands for investigations. " Question time," in spite of the qualms it gives Ministers, and the money it costs taxpayers, is certainly one of the chief excellencies of the British Parliament. It is as essential as an escape valve upon a steam boiler.

Every day that the House convenes an opportunity is given at the commencement of the day, for a period not exceeding an hour, for any member to address questions, not exceeding four, to the several Ministers. As a general thing, all questions must be presented sufficiently in advance that they may be entered upon the printed " Orders of the Day." No question is supposed to include " argument, inference, imputa-

---

44 Below, Chap. vii.

tion, epithet, or ironical expression." Those which do come near this category may be ruled out by the Speaker.

In a single day as many as two hundred and fifty questions, or an average of one hundred and twenty-five, may be answered. The result is not only the one most readily apparent. Everyone will admit that questioning keeps the Ministry and the minor officialdom "on its toes," and serves to check the almost inevitable tendency toward bureaucracy and its concomitant evils. But after all what makes for fewer investigations and consequently less expenditure of funds is the daily questioning which gives the Opposition a chance to "let off steam." This opportunity gives them assurance that their constituents will hear enough of the reverberations to know that, to change the figure, the inquisitorial hand has been doing its work, without the necessity of ransacking the opposing party's family closet for the crumbling skeleton of dead years' "suspicions of malfeasance or of wanton corruption."

The "question," however, is but "the first line of attack." If a member thinks the reply of a Minister too evasive, he may employ a more potent weapon in the form of supplementary questions. This amounts to a cross-examination of the Minister, or inquisition in its more normal character. If the Minister cannot satisfy the Opposition through subsequent answers another recourse remains.

At the close of the questions, any member may arise and ask permission, "to move the adjournment of the House on a matter of urgent public importance." This motion is, in effect, a vote of censure on some particular Minister or on the Government as a whole. Adjournment at an irregular time, following such an attack, is interpreted as imposing an obligation upon the Minister or Government to resign.

The French custom of interpellation differs from the simple English question in being debatable, and in precipitating a vote which may lead to a change of the Ministry. Probably this fact, coupled with the simple question, accounts in considerable measure for the circumstance that investigations have been few and of recent origin in the government of France.

One means of obtaining information in France, short of investigation, arises under the statute of 1910. This Act provides that there must be published by the executive department every five years a statement containing documents, statistics, and details concerning the intimate conduct of the departments. In 1906 a statute was passed which made it possible for each House to appoint two members to investigate conditions in the War and Marine Departments periodically. Moreover, it is definitely stipulated by law that either the Chamber or Senate may authorize committees to make inquiries into executive acts whenever, in their opinion, the need arises.[45] In 1914, for the first time in history, power was given to Parliamentary committees to compel the attendance of witnesses during an investigation. The same law fixes a penalty for failure of witnesses to appear and take oath.[46]

Importance Attached to Investigations by German Constitution.—The new German Constitution places great importance upon investigations as a salutary method of obtaining information and enforcing responsibility. Indications are, if the present frequency of investigations continues in Germany, that they will be accorded as much significance as in the United States. The writer believes that were the governments of Germany and the United States as efficiently coordinated as those of England and France, investigations would be no more needed in the former cases than in the latter.

Article 34 of the German Constitution provides as follows: " The Reichstag has the right, and on proposal of one-fifth of its members, the duty to appoint committees of investigation." These committees, in public sittings, inquire into the evidence which they, or the proponents, consider necessary. The public may be excluded by a two-thirds vote of the com-

---

[45] Eugene Pierre, Traité de droit politique, électoral, et parlementaire, Secs. 544-596.

[46] Edward M. Sait, Government and Politics of France, 234, 235.

mittee of investigation. The rules of procedure regulate the proceedings of the committee and determine the number of its members.

" The judicial and administrative authorities are required to comply with requests by those committees for information, and the record of the authorities shall on request be submitted to them. The provisions of the code of criminal procedure apply as far as is suitable to the inquiries of these committees and of the authorities assisting them, but the secrecy of letter and other post, telegraph, and telephone services will remain inviolate."

All members of the Reichstag enjoy immunity from being investigated, and from being made to testify, unless the Reichstag chooses to withdraw such immunity.[47] Investigations are conducted in conformity with the Reichstag's rules as concerns internal procedure and organization, and in accordance with the code of criminal procedure as regards outside investigations.

It need hardly be suggested that the only acid test of this scheme of investigations lies in the way actual practice will work out the details. At least one thing appears to one immediately. It is certainly a very liberal stipulation to make investigations upon any subject possible by only one-fifth of the membership of the Reichstag desiring it. In practice, of course, this apparent liberty will probably be restricted in large measure.

To begin with, committees are no longer elected by lot as formerly, where sometimes it was possible for minority blocs to control committees. At present all committees are filled according to proportional representation. That is, each party having over fifteen members is entitled to as many members on every committee as it has delegates proportionately to the

---

[47] Article 38, new German Constitution. For the history of investigations in Germany and for the most important decisions concerning them by the Staatsgerichtshof, see Johannes Mattern, Principles of the Constitutional Jurisprudence of the German Republic, Chap. vii, section entitled " Decisions in Controversies Arising within a State " (Johns Hopkins Press, 1928).

whole number of the Reichstag. Obviously the majority party will be given a majority of every committee. It is possible with a committee so constituted that the findings might be suppressed or badly colored by the majority members. Examination of the investigations of the first four years, however, seems to indicate that in almost every case the power to make the particular investigation was questioned, but after it was once ordered the results appear to have been satisfactory to the minority.[48] These investigations have been marked by a bitter partisan note, with the Socialists especially aggressive. It appears that if investigations of this kind do become numerous there are at least two possible drawbacks to be faced: too many investigations are not conducive to the smooth and efficient ordering of either legislatures or of the administration, and American experience has found them very expensive.

General Summary.—Before turning to the origin of the investigative power in England and its later influence, it is important to recapitulate the chief points brought out in our

---

[48] Examples of the early investigations under the new German Constitution may be found in "Jahrbuch des Offentlichen Rechts," Band xiii (1925), pp. 121-123. The following are examples:

1. Der Untersuchungsausschuss zur Erörterung der Kriegsschuld.
2. . . . "der die gegen den Reichsernährungsminister Hermes erhobenen Vorwürfe zu prüfen hat."
3. . . . "der mit der Untersuchung des Unglücks aus Zeche Mont Cenis beauftragt wird."
4. . . . "zur Feststellung der Ursachen des Massenunglucks in Oppau."
5. . . . "zur Prüfung der unhaltbaren Zustände in den Strafanstalten."
6. . . . "zur Prüfung der Vorwürfe, welche gegen die Reichswehr erhoben worden sind und die Art, wie sie Reichswehrminister erledigt worden sind."
7. . . . "der die Wirksamkeit der von der Reichsregierung und der Reichsbank zur Stützung der Mark getroffenen Massnahmen prüfen und der Vorgänge feststellen soll, die zur Ersshütterung der Stützungsaktion für die Mark auf dem Geldmarkt geführt haben."

Questions raised by investigations are found on pp. 123, 124 of the above report.

development of the nature and extent of the investigative problem in modern constitutional states.

Investigations are studied to best advantage in relation to the legislature because they are an auxiliary agency of the legislative process. Nevertheless the true scope of the investigative power can be appreciated only when the problem is viewed in the light of the complete structure of the government. Investigations have discoverable causes, intimately enmeshed in the fundamental scheme of the government's constitution.

If one were to think of the legislature simply as the law-making organ, he could not grasp the real importance of investigating activity. But a legislature in modern constitutional states has three chief functions, namely, to supervise the administration, to control the expenditure, and to make laws. Incidental functions, such as membership and the formation of public opinion, are also found in legislatures of modern constitutional governments.

The Congress of the United States, although a legislature of specified powers, possesses all the chief and incidental functions appertaining to legislatures in other modern constitutional governments. If there was ever any doubt concerning Congress' power to supervise the executive departments it has been put to rest by a long-continued practice in exercising control over them. Committees of investigation have played a long and important rôle in helping to accomplish this end.

We must recognize three principal functions of Congressional investigating committees, namely, the membership function, the law-making function, and the power of investigating the administration in order to determine whether or not the legislature's will has been carried out lawfully, economically, and efficiently.

In the governments of England, France, and Germany, investigations do not play as important a part as in the United States. Investigations are provided for in the new German constitution and may attain great importance. In England there were at one time many investigations, fulfilling similar functions to those in the United States. The reason for the present disparity is found in the fact that England and France have established machinery of a permanent character to fill the natural functions which investigations might otherwise fulfill. The chief factors working to lessen the number of investigations in either England or France, or both, are, the judicial determination of electoral disputes, Royal Commissions, responsible cabinet government, " grievance before supply," systematic full reports by administrative officials, an efficient budget and accounting system, the parliamentary question, and interpellations. Investigations are not inevitable in a government but may be replaced just as fast as permanent machinery can be installed to meet the same needs.

CHAPTER II

English Origin and Later Influence of the Investigative Power

Importance of English Precedents in Development of the Investigative Power in the United States.—Congressional committees of inquiry were unhesitatingly utilized almost as soon as the Government of the United States began because of the knowledge which members of Congress had of the secure position and the breadth of activity which such committees had long enjoyed in England. Investigating committees have a foundation in Parliamentary custom which rivals the antiquity of most practices still forming a part of the procedure of Parliament or of Congress. The basis of the exercise of the investigative power in both cases therefore is found in custom rather than in a right specifically created by constitutional or statutory provision. The original use and continued exercise of the power were found necessary for legislative self-survival and for efficient legislation.

As a writer has recently pointed out,[1] however, the value of English precedents which relate to investigations has been questioned by authorities deserving careful consideration.[2] It is argued that the comparison is valueless because Parliament was once a judicial body, a High Court, in contrast to Congress, which has always been admittedly legislative; further, "that powers judicial in character commonly exercised by it are attributable to its judicial nature and therefore cannot be incident to a legislature stripped in its creation of all judicial functions." [3]

---

[1] James M. Landis, "Congressional Power of Investigation," Harvard Law Review, XL, No. 2, 153-221. The writer is indebted to Mr. Landis for a large part of the material used in this chapter.

[2] Kilbourn vs. Thompson, 103 U. S. 168 (1880). The view taken by the court is criticised by C. S. Potts, "Power of Legislative Bodies to Punish for Contempt" (1926), 74 U. Pa. L. Rev. 691.

[3] Landis, op. cit., 159; McIlwain, The High Court of Parliament.

Mr. Landis suggests that there are several plausible answers to this contention, which would seem to discountenance the opposing point of view. In the first place, scholars are not uniformly agreed that Parliament was a judicial body. They also argue that " the House of Commons was fundamentally no more a judicial body than the House of Representatives." [4] It is pointed out, moreover, that there is nothing conclusive in the nature of the power or the way it developed historically in either country that marks it as judicial in nature. Rather, it is distinctly ancillary to the legislative function. The investigative power developed with the customs of Parliament. Therefore, the question is not a judicial one, but it is a simple question of procedural development in legislation. Also, the argument assumes there are three sharply defined categories—legislative, executive, and judicial—whereas it is now generally admitted that legislatures possess judicial and executive powers in addition to their legislative powers. Finally, the evidence shows that the origins of legislative committees of inquiry postdate the era, assuming there was one, of the supremacy of the High Court. The beginnings undoubtedly lie in a time when Parliament was the Magna Concilium, untainted by judicial aspects.[5]

There can be no question that Congress adopted the investigative function and that the scope of its exercise was largely determined by reference to English precedents. On the other hand, the legality of Congressional investigations cannot be established by reliance upon such analogies. It was generally believed that English precedents did have legal force until the opposite view was held in Kilbourn *vs.* Thompson. In that important case Mr. Justice Miller concluded his examination of the subject with these words: " We are of opinion that the right of the House of Representatives to punish the citizen for contempt of its authority or breach of its privileges can derive no support from the precedents of the two

---

[4] Potts, op. cit., U. Pa. L. Rev. (1926), pp. 692-700.
[5] See Redlich, Procedure of the House of Commons, I, 24, 25; III, 77, 78 (1908).

Houses of the English Parliament, nor from the adjudged cases in which the English courts have upheld these practices." [6]

Investigations Respecting the Eligibility of Members.—Most writers on English constitutional history place the date of the first investigation in the modern sense of the word about 1571. Since then the investigative power has been steadily employed and greatly broadened. Walter Bagehot, writing near the end of the nineteenth century, said of its scope, " The House of Commons has inquired into most things, but has never had a committee on " the Queen." [7] Probably more investigations have been ordered concerning the eligibility of members than upon any other public question. Thus, for example, in 1571 committees of nine members were appointed to investigate election disputes.[8]   As early as 1581 a committee was appointed for the whole session to deal with all disputed election returns. Not until 1586 did the House actually gain the right to resolve election disputes. Obviously cases of this kind demand the ability of the committee to send for persons and papers.

For example, in the case of Sir Francis Godwin in 1604, the following entry may be found: " Power given in that case to send an Officer, and to view and search any Record or other thing of that kind, which may help their Knowledge or Memory in this particular Service."[9]   D'Ewes records that after 1592 all election disputes were assigned to one and the same large committee, consisting of the privy councillors and thirty or more named members.[10]   Later examples of the expression of the power are not lacking.

Thus in 1833, upon the petition of several Liverpool mer-

---

[6] 103 U. S. 168. This does not dispose of the historical fact, of course, that investigations in the United States owe their origin to Parliamentary counterparts.

[7] W. Bagehot, The English Constitution, 125.

[8] De Lolme, Rise and Progress of the English Constitution, I, 297.

[9] Hale, Original Institutive, Power, and Jurisdiction of Parliaments, 105.

[10] D'Ewes, op. cit., 471.

chants, a committee was appointed to investigate alleged election briberies.[11] During the course of the investigation a woman witness twice refused to testify and was admonished by the Speaker that, even though she feared danger to her life in answering the questions, she must answer them, for upon refusal " she would be committed to the custody of the Sergeant-at-Arms for a breach of the Privileges of the House." [12]

Investigations in Aid of Legislation.—A second chief function of special committees on public matters was to investigate questions of fact and law and report the findings to either house. Throughout, it was often the practice to appoint select committees to act with a committee from the House of Lords to determine such questions. The history of such committees cannot be traced here, but it presents a great variety of matters considered, and the aggregate comprises the most interesting group of investigations.

Such, for example, was the case of Sheriff Acton of London, who was found guilty by the Commons of prevarication before the " Committee for the Examination of the Merchant's Business," and in consequence sentenced to the Tower.[13] Again, on April 21, 1664, a committee, to whom a bill for settling the navigation of the River Wye had been referred, was empowered by the House to send to the Warden of the Fleet to cause James Pitson to be brought before them from time to time and be examined as occasion required.[14]

Investigations of Money Matters.—Shortly after the middle of the 17th Century, Parliament established its undoubted right to control the appropriation and expenditure of public funds. Thereafter the exercise of the investigative power to discover whether funds appropriated had been expended for

---

[11] Power to send for persons and records was granted. 88 Comm. Journal, 144 (1833), op. cit.

[12] D'Ewes, 218. Quoted by Landis, 161, op cit. See also other contempt cases cited by Mr. Landis.

[13] Petyt, Miscellena Parliamentaria (1681), 120.

[14] 8 Comm. Journal, 547 (1664).

4

authorized purposes became a common practice. In 1666, for instance, a committee was commissioned " to inspect the several Accompts of the Officers of the Navy, Ordnance, and Stores," with power to send for persons and papers.[15]

With the final supremacy of Parliament in 1688 the last vestige of immunity from financial accountability on the part of royalty was swept away. A year later one discovers Parliament appointing a host of committees to investigate sundry abuses of the exchequer. Outstanding among these were searching inquiries into alleged incompetencies in the conduct of the war in Ireland. On June 1, 1689, a committee was appointed " to inquire who has been the Occasion of the Delays in sending Relief over Ireland, and particularly to Londonderry." [16] Five months later a committee was created to determine, " By what means the Intelligence came to be given to their Majesties Enemies, concerning the several Stations of Winter Guards of their Majesties Navy; and the Transportation of the Army; and all other Things relating to the War, both by Sea and Land, the last year." [17] Both committees were granted power to send for persons and papers.

Investigations Respecting Public Administrative Agencies.—With frequent investigations to control the expenditure of public funds, there arose inquiries to supervise administrative agencies and their personnel. On November 6, 1689, a committee was appointed, with power to send for persons and papers, to inquire into the report that a commissioner of the East India Company had proclaimed martial law, without warrant, in " Sancta Hellena." [18]

---

[15] Ibid., p. 628.

[16] 10 Comm. Journal, 162 (1689).

[17] Ibid., 278. Hallam says of these committees: " I do not think there is any earlier precedent in the Journals for so specific an inquiry into the conduct of a public officer, especially a military command—No courtier has ever since ventured to deny this general right of inquiry, though it is a frequent practice to elude it. The right to inquire draws with it the necessary means. . . . " Const. Hist. of Eng." (5th ed.), 570.

[18] 10 Comm. Journal, 280.

In 1729 the administration of prisons became the subject of investigation. Accordingly on March 10, 1729, Mr. Oglethorpe, " from the Committee, appointed to enquire into the State of the Gaols of this Kingdom, acquainted the House, that he was directed by the Committee to move the House, that they may have Power to examine any Persons they shall think fit, in the most solemn Manner. Ordered, That the said Committee be impowered to examine any Persons, they shall think fit, in the most solemn Manner." [19]

Similarly, two years later an investigation became the means of revealing scandals in the administration of poor relief by a corporation created for such a purpose. In this case the committee soon discovered that the principal witnesses were prepared to flee the country because of the revelations bound to follow. To insure the effectiveness of the investigation, the House thereupon ordered the arrest of witnesses pending their examination; [20] authority to search for books and papers was granted.[21] Witnesses proven guilty of prevarication before the committee were imprisoned for their contempt of the power of the House.[22]

The great object which was always suggested as the basis of all manifestations of the investigative power was the legislative one. It is not as readily cognizable in some cases as in others, but the underlying necessity is patent. An instance of the legislative purpose clearly stated appears in the following. In the Commons Journal for February 17, 1728, it is:

Ordered, That the Committee, appointed to inspect what Laws are expired, or near expiring, and to report their Opinion to the House, which of them are fit to be revived, or continued, and who are instructed to inspect the Laws relating to Bankrupts, and consider what Alterations are proper to be made therein, have Power to send for Persons, Papers, and Records, with respect to that Instruction.[23]

---

[19] Ibid., 488 (1729).
[20] Ibid., pp. 800-801 (1731).
[21] Ibid., p. 843.
[22] Ibid., 810, 811, 842, 852, 910, 913, 914, 915. For other cases of this character see Alpheus Todd, Parliamentary Government in England, I, 423-428.
[23] 21 Comm. Journal, 223 (1728).

Recent Cases of Investigations.—Coming down to fairly recent cases of outstanding investigations of the character noted above, Redlich mentions the following: Imprisonment of a Member, 1902; Sale of Intoxicating Liquors to Children Bill, 1901; the Future Civil List of the Sovereign, 1901; the Cottage Homes Bill, 1899; Select Committee on the Aged Deserving Poor, 1899. Additional instances of possible interest to the reader are cited in the footnote.[24]

General Power of Investigation Upheld by the Courts.— " It is hardly worthwhile to enumerate later instances of exercising a right which had become indisputable," [25] wrote Hallam in 1867 concerning Parliament's investigative powers. When the question came to the courts the answer was clear and decisive. Probably the most striking opinion as to Parliament's legal as well as customary right to investigate public questions and summon witnesses was delivered by Lord Coleridge in 1845: [26]

> That the Commons are, in the words of Lord Coke, the general inquisitors of the realm, I fully admit; it would be difficult to define any limits by which the subject matter of their inquiry can be bounded; it is unnecessary to attempt to do so now; I would be content to state that they may inquire into everything which it concerns the public weal for them to know; and they themselves, I think, are entrusted with the determination of what falls within that category. Coextensive with the jurisdiction to inquire must be their authority to call for the attendance of witnesses, to enforce it by arrest when disobedience makes that necessary.

---

[24] Redlich, Procedure of the House of Commons, II, 194. The following cases which have arisen since 1776 are mentioned by Landis (op. cit., p. 164, note). The case of Captain Huxley Sandon before the committee charged to investigate the conduct of the Duke of York as commander of the Army (64 Comm. Journal, 15 et. passim (1809); the case of John A. Shee before the committee inquiring into the alleged abuses of patronage of the East India Company (ibid., pp. 100, 102); the case of Lieutenant Colonel Fairman before the committee inquiring into the Orange Institution (90 ibid., 564 passim. 1835); the case of Norman McLean before the committee investigating the conduct of General Darling as governor of New South Wales (ibid., p. 601), and the case of the directors of the Cambrian Railway Company who had discharged an employee because of testimony given a Parliamentary committee (147 ibid., p. 129, 1892).

[25] Hallam, Constitutional History of England (5th ed. 1867), 570.

[26] Howard vs. Gosset, 10 Q. B. pp. 359-380 (1845).

Investigative Power Readily Adopted by Colonies.—It was unquestionably the case that representative assemblies in the Thirteen Colonies came to utilize the power of investigation because they assumed that inasmuch as the power was customary of the legislative process in Parliament, its adoption and exercise was just as proper in the Colonies.[27] The fact that in most of the colonies all legislation was subject to the governor's veto and subject also to disallowance by the English authorities if they saw fit, did not seem to indicate to colonial legislatures that their and Parliament's investigative prerogatives might not be identical.

Two important conclusions are to be gleaned from an examination of investigations during the early American period. In the first place, as already suggested, it is significant that investigations should be so deeply rooted in English experience that the power should be adopted without question in colonial governments. Mr. Potts states, " for three-quarters of a century no case involving the contempt power of a legislative body except Anderson vs. Dunn,[28] reached the higher courts, state or federal." This absence of adjudicated cases strongly suggests that there was a general acquiescence in the exercise of the power to compel testimony, for there was no dearth of contumacious cases in the legislatures which might have found their way into the courts, if the persons concerned and their counsel had thought that relief could be obtained from that source.

A second consideration worthy of particular attention is the fact that the scope and pretences of early colonial or state investigations were not in the least diminished by transference from English soil. A few instances of the nature and scope of these investigations will serve to demonstrate the point.

---

[27] The Maryland Constitution of 1776, provided for investigating committees. Prior to that time, however, the power was purely customary. See Potts, op. cit.; p. 714. Throughout this section the writer has relied chiefly upon the research of Mr. Potts.

[28] 6 Wheaton, 204. (U. S. 1821).

Colonial Investigations Directed Toward the Executive.—
During the Indian War of 1722, the Massachusetts House
of Representatives conducted an investigation which amounted
to a determination by the House to supervise the executive.
The result was an argument with the Governor and the even-
tual victory of the representative assembly. In this case the
House stood upon its right to send for Colonel Walton and
Major Moody, the heads of the colonial force in Maine, to
determine responsibility for the failure to carry out certain
offensive operations which the House had authorized at a
previous session. It was readily admitted that the House
could not remove military officials, but nevertheless they held
it, "not only their Privilege but Duty to demand of any
Officer in the pay and service of this Government an account
of his Management while in the Public Employ." [29] Many
witnesses were summoned and Walton and Moody were finally
retired from the service.

Another example of the exercise of the investigative power
with purpose to focus attention upon the conduct of public
officials, in which there seems to be great doubt of legislative
intent, arose in early Pennsylvania history. In this case the
House of Delegates desired to summon witnesses in an action
against W. Moore, Judge of the Court of Common Pleas.
Only the Governor had the power of removal, but nevertheless the House was convinced of its privileges and duty.
After many witnesses had been examined, the House of Delegates respectfully petitioned the Governor to remove the
objectionable official. [30]

*Colonial Investigations Respecting Elections and Public
Finances.*—Colonial counterparts of English investigating
committees with intent to examine elections or the accounts
of public officials are found in most of the Colonies. In Pennsylvania, for instance, the Assembly summoned witnesses in
1742 to consider riots which had occurred at an election. At

---

[29] Journal, I, 165.
[30] Potts, op. cit., 710-711.

the completion of the testimony the Assembly requested the Governor to direct the courts to look into the affair and punish the wrong-doers. Apparently at no time was any intention expressed other than the request in which the investigation culminated. Pennsylvania also had a committee appointed by the Assembly to sit during recess, with " Full Power and Authority to send for Persons, Papers and Records by the Sergeant at Arms of this House, in order that all the said public accounts be fully settled and made ready to be laid before the House on the first Day of their Meeting in September next." [31] An investigating committee clothed with similar powers by the colonial assembly of North Carolina ordered the receiver of powder money at Roanoke, after he had refused a like request from the Governor, to submit his accounts to the House.[32]

Reliance of States upon Investigations.—The stress of Revolution seems not to have diminished the reliance the States put in investigations. In 1781 the Virginia House of Delegates gave its standing committees on religion, privileges and elections, courts of justice, and trade, power "to send for persons, papers, and records for their information." [33] In 1824 the New York Assembly appointed a committee to discover whether the charter of the Chemical Bank had been obtained by corrupt means, and punished a witness, Caldwell, for contumacy.[34]

When the power of state legislatures was at length challenged, the courts were just as decisive in supporting the exercises of the legislature's prerogative as were the English courts.[35] In fact, prior to 1880 no state decision denies or curtails the exercise of the investigative power. Judge Daly of New York struck this note as clearly as anyone in the course of his decision in Briggs *vs.* MacKellar when he said:

[31] Ibid.
[32] Ibid., p. 709.
[33] Ibid.
[34] Ibid.
[35] For cases, Landis, op. cit., p. 167.

Where no constitutional limitation or restriction exists, it is competent for either of the two bodies composing the Legislature, to do, in their separate capacity, whatever may be essential to enable them to legislate. . . . It is a well established principle of this parliamentary law, that either house may instigate an investigation having reference to its own organization, the conduct or qualification of its members, its proceedings, rights, or privileges or any matter affecting the public interest upon which it may be important that it should have exact information, and in respect to which it would be competent for it to legislate. . . . In American legislatures the investigation of public matters before committees, preliminary to legislation, or with the view of advising the house appointing the committee, is, as a parliamentary usage, as well established as it is in England, and the right of either house to compel witnesses to appear and testify before its committees, and to punish for disobedience, has been frequently enforced. . . . The right of inquiry, I think, extends to other matters in respect to which it may be necessary, or may be deemed advisable to apply for legislative aid.[36]

Therefore it is not to be wondered at that three years after the first Congress met, the power of general investigation was vigorously asserted as one of its prerogatives. The members of early Congresses unquestionably attached great significance to the customary powers of the English Parliament, but they drew even more upon their own experience in colonial and early state legislatures. From the powers and prerogatives of the English Parliament and from their own state legislatures, they took over in toto the investigative power. That power consisted of three functions, namely, investigations relative to the legislature's members, investigations in aid of the law-making process, and investigations respecting the financial and ministerial conduct of public servants of the government.

---

[36] Briggs vs. MacKellar, 2 Abb. Pr. 30 (N. Y. 1855), pp. 41, 55-67.

CHAPTER III

INVESTIGATIONS WITH REFERENCE TO MEMBERS OF CONGRESS

Number and Nature of Congressional Investigations.— Congress has utilized its inquisitorial power by appointing investigating committees approximately three hundred and thirty times since the adoption of the Constitution.[1] Beginning with a searching inquiry into the causes of failure of the expedition under General St. Clair in 1792, Congress has since employed the power to ferret out such information as it deemed necessary for any of its purposes. Of the total number of investigations, about one hundred and ninety have been authorized by the House, one hundred and twenty-five have been conducted by the Senate, and fifteen have been the work of joint committees.

An illuminating political history of the United States is written in the records of these committees. Almost any outstanding happening or movement in American history one might mention has been inquired into directly or indirectly by congressional investigating committees. The administration of only one war, the Spanish American, has escaped their surveillance. All of the administrative departments except two, namely, the Departments of Commerce and Labor since their separation in 1913, have been frequently investigated. Scarcely has there been an administrative department established or altered in which a congressional investigating committee did not either reveal the need of, or specifically recommend such action. For example, the creation of the Federal Printing Office was obviously the culmination of a large

---

[1] In arriving at this figure the writer made a careful examination of the records of Congress from 1789 to the end of the Sixty-Ninth Congress. This includes only investigations actually concluded by report or resolution. There is every reason to suppose that I have missed some cases of investigation and that the real number is even larger than suggested. Mr. George Galloway arrived at the conclusion that there have been 285 investigations (George Galloway, " Investigative Function of Congress," Am. Pol. Sci. Rev., XXI, No. 1, 47, Feb., 1927).

number of investigations concerning printing done for the government. Great administrative reforms, like that of the Civil Service, have been aided by the reports of investigating committees.

Two periods, namely the presidencies of Grant and Harding, stand out preëminently as eras when the inquisitorial hand was forced the hardest, and forsooth it is little to be wondered at. No period in American history has been without investigations. From 1789-1814 Congress conducted approximately thirty investigations. Only three of these were attributable to the Senate. In the same length of time, from 1900-1925, Congress conducted about sixty investigations. During this period approximately twenty were attributable to the House, and forty to the Senate. This tendency for the Senate to become the inquisitorial body gains headway each year. Far from being merely a conservative "assembly of old men and elders," as originally expected, the Senate has proved itself the vitriolic critic and persistent regulator of the government.

It appears that until 1827 Congress conducted investigations solely through the agency of select committees, but in that year a standing committee, while inquiring into proposals for pending tariff legislation,[2] was given power to send for persons and papers. Until almost the end of the nineteenth century select committees, ranging from three to fifteen in membership, usually seem to have been preferred for the business of investigation. Since then, however, the policy of giving standing committees investigative powers has met with increasing approval. In less than one-eighth of the total number of cases examined by the writer, has the power to send for persons, papers, or both, not been granted either in authorizing the investigation, or at some time during its course. In these cases the granting of such power was not objected to but it was thought useless unless later found necessary. In

---

[2] Cong. Debates, 20th Cong., 1st sess. 862, 2472. For a history of standing committees, see L. G. McConachie, Congressional Committees, 40-42 (N. Y., 1898).

the past two score years there has been an increasing tendency to authorize investigating committees of the Senate to continue over the adjournment of Congress.

Constitutional Bases of Investigations of this Nature.—In the following three chapters we shall consider separately each of the three functions fulfilled by congressional investigating committees. In this chapter we shall consider the manner in which investigations are employed in pursuance of Congress' membership function.

This class of investigations has its foundation in definite constitutional provisions. Article I, Section 5, Clauses 1 and 2 of the Constitution provide that, " each House shall be the judge of the elections, returns, and qualifications of its own members." Further it is stated that, " Each House may determine the Rules of its proceedings, punish its members for disorderly behaviour, and, with the concurrence of two-thirds, expel a member." From these provisions have sprung investigations with the purpose of determining the qualification or conduct of members of Congress. A further provision of the Constitution (Art. I, Sec. 6, Cl. 1) states the immunities of members, providing that, " They shall in all cases, except treason, felony and breach of the peace, be privileged from arrest during their attendance at the same; and for any speech or debate in any other place." It has been declared that the latter part of this provision especially should be liberally construed.[3] Several investigations have arisen upon questions of privilege, concerning the immunity of members or of contempts against the dignity of either chamber of Congress.

Consequently we shall consider three classes of investigations in the remainder of this chapter, namely, investigation of the qualifications of members, of their conduct and behavior, and of breaches of the immunity of members or of the dignity of either of the Houses.

---

[3] C. K. Burdick, Law of the American Constitution, 176. See also Coffin vs. Coffin (1808), 4 Mass. 1; Kilbourn vs. Thompson (1881), 103 U. S. 168.

Investigations Concerning the Qualifications of Members.—
The largest number of investigations relating to the membership of the two Houses of Congress are those respecting the qualification of members. Many investigations of this character might be cited. However, they are recorded in the "Contested Election" reports of the Congresses, beginning with the year 1789. In the early period many of these investigations were conducted by select committees of the two Houses, but of recent years the uniform practice has been to make such inquiries through the medium of subcommittees of the Committee on Privileges and Elections. The only contested election cases which we have deemed to be within our present consideration are those in which power was granted the committee to send for persons and papers.

One of the most interesting of these cases arose in 1844 concerning the affairs of Rhode Island. Originally the investigation was ordered with the express purpose of determining the qualifications of Representatives seeking to be sworn into office.[4] The ultimate scope of the committee's report included a consideration of the general conditions of the state, and of the part the President had taken in the affairs there. Identically the same thing was true in regard to the comprehensive Howard investigation of affairs in Kansas in 1856.[5]

The particular questions of eligibility which investigating committees have delved into under this constitutional power have differed appreciably. Some of the questions raised border upon the ludicrous. For instance, in 1844 the Senate considered it not only fitting, but apparently quite indispensable, to inquire into the mental qualifications of Senator-elect J. M. Niles, of Connecticut.[6] In defense of his motion for this investigation Mr. Jarnagin, the mover, stated that, "It was due to the people . . . to the Senate . . . to ascer-

---

[4] Cong. Record, 26th Cong. 1st sess. 158, 299.
[5] 34th Cong. 1st sess., H. R. Rept. No. 200.
[6] 28th Cong. 1st sess. 592, 593. As finally amended, reference to mental qualification was struck out (ibid., p. 593).

tain whether the afflictions of this gentleman were such as rendered him eligible as a Senator." On May 16th the committee appointed to make the investigation reported that after questioning witnesses, among them medical men, they had come to the conclusion that the Senator-elect was not of " unsound mind," and that although he was " laboring under mental and physical debility " it was their opinion that " participating at least two hours a day actively in its [the Senate's] business will be the means of usefulness and a resource against disease." [7] The committee's recommendation that Niles be permitted to take his seat was accordingly adopted.[8]

Most of the outstanding investigations of late years, in reference to the qualification of members, have been concerned primarily with " excessive and illegal expenditure of money " in elections.   Foremost among such instances was the Newberry case in the Sixty-seventh Congress,[9] and the charges of stupendous expenditures by Senators-elect Vare and Smith, of Pennsylvania and Illinois, respectively, brought to light by the Reed investigations.[10]

Investigations Respecting the Behavior of Members.—One of the most comprehensive uses of the investigative power to inquire into the behavior of members of Congress is found in

---

[7] Ibid., p. 636.

[8] Ibid.

[9] 67th Cong. 1st sess., Sen. Rep. No. 277; Cong. Record, 69th Cong. 1st sess., 9678, 12018, 12840.

[10] The Vare and Smith investigations were nothing short of a political master-stroke on the part of Reed. Mr. Reed succeeded in passing a resolution for not only an investigation of the general election, but also of the primaries. Frank R. Kent says of this: " Unquestionably the disclosures of Reed under this resolution constitute the most remarkable single-handed achievement of any public man in the last six years. Merely to get such a resolution through the Senate at any time and under any conditions would not have been easy. Regardless of their politics, Senators do not care for investigating committees that investigate Senators. For a Democratic Senator to have got it through a Republican Senate when it was clear the investigation meant a ripping open of Republican wounds and a devastating exposure of Republican methods is so unusual that it is hard to think of a precedent." Senator " Jim " Reed, in The Forum, LXXVIII, No. 1 (July, 1927), p. 67.

the colorful inquiry of 1812,[11] in which it was alleged that the secrecy of the House had been violated. On April 3, 1812, a committee was appointed in the House " to inquire whether there has been any, and if any, what violation of the secrecy imposed by this House during the present session as to certain of its proceedings. . . ." Power was given to summon witnesses and send for papers. The alleged violation of secrecy had been reported in a Georgetown paper called the " Spirit of Seventy-six." It was alleged that proceedings concerning the embargo, which had taken place behind closed doors, had been permitted to be published in said paper, through the culpability of members of the House, before secrecy had been removed.

The committee discovered that one Rounsavell, an editor of the Alexandria Herald, had supplied the information.[12] Debate on whether to summon him occupied two days in the House. Ultimately Rounsavell appeared but refused to answer certain questions put by the committee. He was brought to the bar of the House, purged of contempt by expressing readiness to testify, and released. The committee finally reported that no members were sufficiently compromised by the charges to recommend punishment or action by the House.[13]

Of greater political significance and more condemnatory in character were charges brought forward by the " Daily

---

[11] Ann. Cong., 12th Cong. part 1, pp. 1600, 1617. There were two outstanding cases prior to this which deserve mention. Proceedings were brought in 1808 to expel John Smith from the Senate for being a party to the Aaron Burr conspiracy. Burr was tried for treason and acquitted. Therefore two thirds of the Senate could not be brought to concur in Smith's expulsion (See Taft's Senate Election Cases, 79). Prior to this, in 1797. there was a famous investigation which resulted in Senator William Blount losing his seat. He was expelled on charges of stirring up the Indians and of interfering with the work of the government agents among them. (Reference to this investigation is found in Annals of Congress, 5th Cong., I, 31, 461; II, 2319. See also Taft's Cases, 74).

[12] Hinds' Precedents, III, 103.

[13] Ann. Cong., 12th Cong., part I, 1255, 1263, 1587. Rounsavell admitted overhearing the conversation of certain Representatives in the Capitol corridors.

Times," of Washington City, in four different daily editions of March, 1846. The country was at fever pitch over the Oregon controversy. War seemed imminent. Some favored compromise, but the majority in Congress were pledged to an unswerving independent attitude. Charges appearing in the Times asserted that caucuses had been held by Whig Senators to favor compromise, and that at some of them direct negotiation had been had with the British Minister.

One article stated, among other things, " If this combination between the British Minister as one part, and a few recreant Democratic Senators joined with a majority of the Whig Senators, succeeds in its settled plot, the administration will be driven from its mission . . . confusion will reign triumphant, President Polk will be left without a party, and British rapacity will feed upon American treachery. . . . Look to the Senate." [14]

On March 12th a special investigating committee of five members of the Senate was appointed, with power to send for persons and papers, in order to determine the truth of the charges.[15] As the chairman later reported, "the committee believed that their researches were to be directed to the truth of the charges of corruption made in said paper with a view to the conduct of the Senate and its members, and not with the view of arraigning or punishing the authors of the publication." [16]

The editors of the paper and several Senators were duly examined. Four days later the committee reported. The libellants, for such they appeared, disclaimed any first hand information of the charges, but said they had been told Daniel Webster was reputed to have made them first.[17] This charge was not corroborated. The committee concluded that the charges were purely libellous, and that neither the conduct nor the reputation of any Senator was sullied.[18]

---

[14] Cong. Globe, 29th Cong., 1st sess., 488, 525.
[15] Ibid.
[16] 29th Cong. 1st sess., Sen. Doc. No. 222, vol. V.
[17] Ibid., pp. 1-32.
[18] Ibid., p. 32.

By far one of the most outstanding investigations of this kind, judged by its convictions, was a sweeping investigation in 1857 of corrupt combinations of members within the House.[19]   Charges to the effect that between twenty-five and thirty members of the House habitually voted according to instructions from commercial interests who bribed them to vote as a unit, were advertised widely in a series of articles written by its Washington correspondent for the " New York Times." After a gruelling cross-examination at the hands of the select committee the Times correspondent admitted there were only four members whom he had definite information against.   The select committee of five members, appointed January 9th, 1857, rendered its report and recommendations on February 19th.[20]

The committee moved that William A. Gilbert, representative from New York, should be expelled for having accepted considerations to secure the adoption of a certain book and the passage of the Iowa land bill.[21]   William Welch, member from Connecticut, was found guilty of accepting bribes in the case of an Invalid Pension claim.[22]   Francis Edwards, from a district in New York, was alleged and found to be guilty of offering pecuniary inducement to another member of the House for his vote on a Minnesota land grant.[23]   In the remaining case, as in the former cases, the committee advocated to the House the expulsion of the recreant member. Not only did the accused, O. B. Matteson, a member from New York, accept and offer bribes to abet the passage of the Des Moines grant resolution, but he had defamed the character of the House by a wilful libel to the effect that a large number of members were likewise customary recipients of bribes.[24]

The importance of this investigation is further enhanced

---

[19] Cong. Globe, 34th Cong., 3rd sess., pp. 277, 404.
[20] 34th Cong., 3rd sess., H. R. Rept. No. 404.
[21] Ibid., p. 9.
[22] Ibid., p. 14.
[23] Ibid., p. 19.
[24] Ibid., p. 26.

by the fact that the Act of 1857, making contumacy before Congressional committees a criminal offense punishable by indictment and prosecution according to regular criminal procedure,[25] was the immediate consequence of the refusal of J. W. Simonton, the Times reporter, to testify.[26] The penalty of Simonton's gross exaggeration was permanent expulsion from the chamber.[27]

Among more recent investigations of this character, mention should be made of the Credit Mobilier scandal of 1871,[28] the politically significant " Silver Pool Investigation " of 1891,[29] alleged bribery by the sugar interests in the tariff of 1894,[30] alleged graft in Postoffice leasing, 1903,[31] the connection of certain members with the ship subsidy lobby in 1910,[32] the charges against Senator Wheeler, 1924,[33] and charges of corrupt practice against Representatives Zihlman, of Maryland, and John W. Langley, of Kentucky, in the same year.[34]

Immunity of Members.—The investigation par excellence which demonstrates the use which may be made of the investigative power as an adjunct to the constitutional stipulation concerning the immunity of members, is the case of the assault upon Senator Charles Sumner, in 1856.[35] Sumner,

---

[25] 11 Stat. at L., 155 (1857). This became Pars. 102-104 Rev. Stat.

[26] On January 21, 1857, Orr, a member of the committee, introduced a resolution for the arrest of Simonton, to answer as for a contempt, and also appended a bill making such contumacy a criminal offense. The purpose of the bill was " to inflict a greater punishment than the committee believes the House possesses the power to inflict." Resolution and bill passed the House by a vote of 163 to 12, and the Senate by a vote of 46 to 3. Cf. Landis, op. cit., 186.

[27] Report, op. cit., 38.

[28] Below, Chap. V.

[29] Cong. Rec., 51st Cong., 2nd sess., pp. 1208, 1470, H. Rept. No. 4006.

[30] Cong. Rec., 53rd Cong., 2nd sess., pp. 4796, 4851, Sen. Repts. Nos. 436, 457, 477, 485.

[31] Cong. Rec., 58th Cong., 1st sess., H. Rept. No. 237.

[32] Cong. Rec., 61st Cong., 1st sess., pp. 4016, H. Rept. No. 2297.

[33] Cong. Rec., 68th Cong. 1st sess., pp. 5995, Sen. Rept. No. 537.

[34] Ibid., p. 8653, H. Res. No. 217.

[35] Cong. Globe, 34th Cong., 1st sess., pp. 1279, 1317.

5

it is well known, had been mercilessly beaten upon the head by a member of the House. Immediately following the attack, the Senate passed certain resolutions which stated, in part, " That this assault was a breach of the privileges of the Senate. . . . That the Senate, for a breach of its privileges, cannot arrest a member of the House of Representatives, and, a fortiori, cannot try and punish him; that such authority devolves upon the House of which he is a member." [36]

Accordingly on May 23, 1856, a select committee was appointed in the House with power to take testimony under oath, and submit resolutions of recommendation.[37] As to the constitutional question involved the committee stated in its report, rendered June 2nd, that the attack " was a breach of the privileges not only of the Senate, but of the Senator assailed, and of this House, as a coördinate branch of the legislative department of government, in direct violation of the Constitution of the United States, which declares that Senators and Representatives, " for any speech or debate in either House shall not be questioned in any other place." [38]

It was shown from testimony that the attack was occasioned by a powerful address which Sumner had delivered a few days previously in the Senate. Therefore the committee stated that, " The act cannot, therefore, be regarded otherwise than as an aggravated assault upon the inestimable right of freedom of speech guaranteed by the Constitution." [39]

The committee concluded with the recommendation that Preston S. Brooks, the assaulter, " be, and he is forthwith, expelled from this House as a Representative from the state of South Carolina," and further, that the House express its disapprobation of those members of the House who might have interfered in Sumner's behalf but apparently sympathized with the intentions of the assailant.[40] Two of the five members of the committee submitted a minority view in

---

[36] 34th Cong., 1st sess., H. Rept. No. 182.
[37] Cong. Globe, 34th Cong., 1st sess., p. 1279.
[38] 34th Cong., 1st sess., H. Rept. No. 182, p. 4.
[39] Ibid., p. 3.
[40] Ibid., p. 5.

which they denied the House's jurisdiction over the alleged assault.[41] The majority report was not adopted, but Brooks resigned almost immediately thereafter.

Similar in the gravity of the wound inflicted, but differing in the station of the individual committing the aggression, was an attack upon Representative William D. Kelley, of Pennsylvania, by a citizen of Louisiana, in 1865.[42] On January 20th, the House raised a committee of three members because " it is understood that on the evening of Friday, the 20th ultimo, A. P. Field, a citizen of Louisiana, did attempt, by language of intimidation and bullying to deter William D. Kelley, a representative in this House . . . from the free and fearless exercise of his rights and duties as a member of Congress and from voting and deciding upon a pending subject of legislation . . . thus committing a breach of the privilege of this House." [43]

It was discovered that the attack had occurred in Willard's Hotel, Washington, D. C. The assailant had alleged that Kelley was opposing legislation which would admit him to a seat in the House. Kelley expressed ignorance. There were words, and then Field struck Kelley with a pocketknife, producing a serious wound. He also threatened to shoot Kelley.[44] The committee unanimously resolved that the assailant should be apprehended under a warrant by the Sergeant-at-arms, and that so much of the resolution granting the privilege of being seated to the claimants from the State of Louisiana as applies to A. P. Field, should be rescinded.[45]

An instance where an investigation was ordered purely in response to a question of personal privilege on the part of a Senator, and where the reputation of the House or Senate was not raised in support of the power, is afforded in the case of Senator Charles Dietrich, of Nebraska. On February 1st, 1904, Dietrich requested as a matter of personal privilege

---

[41] Ibid., p. 19.
[42] Cong. Globe, 38th Cong., 2nd sess., pp. 371, 644.
[43] 38th Cong., 2nd sess., H. Rept. No. 10.
[44] Ibid., p. 13.
[45] Ibid., p. 3.

that, inasmuch as his reputation as a Senator and a representative of his State had been questioned by a grand jury indictment in Omaha, a select committee should be appointed to consider and report upon the case.[46]

Process had been had against Dietrich before the grand jury at Omaha, Neb., on charges of bribery in securing the appointment of a postmaster, and of corruption in leasing private property to the government, both in his capacity as Senator-elect.[47] Since the date of the charges alleged was prior to Dietrich's taking the oath of office, a verdict of acquittal was directed by Circuit Judge Van Devanter.[48] However, Dietrich gave as the reason for his motion that, "If guilty of the least of these charges, I deserve to be driven from this high place in disgrace and receive the severest penalty of the criminal law. Confident in my innocence, I desire to submit the whole matter to the Senate." [49] On April 14th Mr. Platt from the committee presented the report of the committee,[50] which found that, "Upon full consideration of all the evidence, the committee is of opinion that Senator Dietrich has not been guilty of any violation of the statutes of the United States or of any corrupt or unworthy conduct."

Disadvantages in the System.—In the foregoing survey of congressional investigating activity respecting the eligibility, conduct, and immunity of members, of necessity only a few examples could be given. The cases with which we have dealt were chosen primarily because they are typical of the great number of such investigations.

The importance which investigations of this character may assume is not readily overestimated. The time they consume in the opening days of Congress is alarming. A situation, which always has been objectionable, has been even more com-

---

[46] Cong. Rec., 52nd Cong., 2nd sess., p. 1447.
[47] This was a case of alleged conspiracy under Section 1781, Rev. Stat.
[48] Hinds, op. cit., III, 157.
[49] Ibid., 156.
[50] Cong. Rec., 52nd Cong., 2nd sess., pp. 4800, 4801. Cf. the case of Senator Kerr, of Indiana, in Hinds, III, Par. 1853.

plicated of recent years by frequent investigations concerning the expenditures of Congressmen-elect. Such cases are sure to be dealt with by investigating committees, and when the committees report, the ensuing battle in the House is liable to be fought, long, bitterly, and with " the inherent frailty of politicians " to treat the contest as one of political strength.

Nowhere is the disorder to which the present system is exposed more glaringly apparent than in the dispute arising over the election of Frank L. Smith as a Senator from Illinois in 1926. The facts of the case, briefly stated, are as follows:

Smith was elected a Senator from Illinois for a term of six years commencing March 4, 1927.[51] When Senator McKinley, the incumbent, died suddenly in December, 1926, Governor Small of Illinois, in accordance with the Constitution and the laws of Illinois, appointed Smith to fill the vacancy. Smith's credentials were presented to the Senate by Senator Deneen of Illinois, on January 19, 1927, and Smith himself was ready to take the oath on that day.

In the period between the primary and the general election, however, a select committee of the Senate, with Senator Reed of Missouri at the head, was dispatched to Illinois to investigate alleged illegal expenditures by Smith in the primary campaign. As in the case of the Vare investigation in Pennsylvania, comprehensive powers bestowed upon the committee made it possible for them to investigate the Illinois primary campaign. It was soon learned that $250,000, or one-half of Smith's campaign fund, had been contributed by Samuel Insull, a wealthy public utilities operator.

The Committee on Privileges and Elections failed to report before the end of the session on March 4.[52] As a result, for more than two months the State of Illinois was represented

---

[51] Ex-Senator James W. Wadsworth presents some interesting phases of the case in " The Senate or the States," in North Amer. Rev., No. 838 (Dec. 1927), 593.

[52] As the writer recounts this case, December, 1927, it appears inevitable that Illinois shall continue with only one-half representation in the Senate for an indefinite period.

by only one Senator. Irrespective of the merits of Smith's qualifications, and of the Senate's right to bar him on the basis of the evidence presented, it plainly appears to the writer that such a dilatory system is badly in need of reform.

Under the present English system such a delay is usually obviated by the judicial hearing of the case. Such a plan appears eminently advisable for the United States. Under such a system a court would exercise the substance of the power, in making the opinion, leaving each house its constitutional right to enact the final decision by a vote, or to overrule the opinion of the court. Such a reversal happens rarely in England, and there is no reason for supposing it would happen more frequently in the United States. It is thought that this plan is thoroughly in consonance with the separation of powers doctrine of the United States.[53] It is simply fol-

---

[53] Of course it would be unconstitutional for Congress to attempt to give a court of federal jurisdiction the power to make final decision of election cases. The power to decide cases in which the qualifications of members is involved cannot be delegated. Nor would it be valid for Congress to give such a court power to decide cases which might later be reversed by action of one of the Houses. Gordon vs. U. S. (2 Wallace, 561, 117 U. S. 697) is authority for these views. However it is thought that validity would attach to a plan whereby Congress might establish an inferior federal court, which would have power to give electoral opinions, as distinguished from decisions. The particular House would then accept or reverse the opinion, according to the system of the English Parliament. Under such a plan there would be no appeal to the Supreme Court. The Court of Claims now performs an analogous function for Congress and its committees (See Act of March 3, 1883, 22 Stat. 485. Also comment by Burdick, The Law of the American Constitution, 138, 139).

Again, there would seem to be no legal objection, and there might be possible advantages, in establishing a joint commission of members and of federal judges, such body to have only advisory power concerning election disputes. (The question of whether Congress might appoint duly appointed judges to act as claims commissioners was raised, but not decided, in United States vs. Ferreira, 13 Howard, 40, 1851).

Under an earlier Act of 1792, however, all of the judges seemed to think that if Congress had intended the judges to act as commissioners they might legally have done so. (Notes to Hayburn's Case, 1792, 2 Dallas 409, and United States vs. Ferreira, 1851, 13 Howard 40, 52. The present German plan of deciding disputed elections differs from this proposal chiefly in the fact that it makes the findings of the commission final and irreviewable (Munro, Governments of Europe, 632, 633).

lowing out the policy earlier manifested by Congress in giving the courts jurisdiction of contempts against its investigating committees. It appeals to one because judicial powers should, where possible, be handled by a judicial body, and because of the time it would save both houses of Congress.

As regards the activity of investigating committees respecting the conduct and immunity of members, there is no substitute device readily foreseen. However, the number of investigations of this character are few, and the writer believes there is no adequate reason at the present time for their not being handled by investigating committees.

CHAPTER IV

INVESTIGATIONS AS COLLATERAL TO THE LAW-MAKING FUNCTION

Constitutional Stipulations.—The first article of Section I of the Constitution of the United States provides that, " All legislative powers herein granted shall be vested in a Congress of the United States, which shall consist of a Senate and House of Representatives." The provision " All legislative powers herein granted shall be vested in a Congress " means that Congress, " within the limits of its powers, and observing the restrictions imposed by the Constitution, may in its discretion enact any statute appropriate to accomplish the objects for which the National Government was established." [1]

The last paragraph of Article I, Section VIII, provides that Congress shall have power, " To make all Laws which shall be necessary and proper for carrying into Execution the foregoing Powers, and all other Powers vested by this Constitution in the Government of the United States, or in any Department or Officer thereof." In the recent case of McGrain *vs.* Daugherty, the Supreme Court of the United States decided that the investigative power of Congress is necessary and proper for the execution of the above constitutional stipulations. [2] They say:

A legislative body cannot legislate wisely or effectively in the absence of information respecting the conditions which the legislature is intended to affect or change; and where the legislative body does not itself possess the requisite information—which not infrequently is true—recourse must be had to others who do possess it. Experience has taught that mere requests for such information often are unavailing, and also that information which is volunteered is not always accurate or complete; so some means of compulsion are essential to obtain what is needed. All this was true before and when the Constitution was framed and adopted. In that period the power of inquiry—with enforcing process—was regarded and employed as a necessary and appropriate attribute of the power

---

[1] Burton vs. U. S., 202 U. S. 344.
[2] McGrain vs. Daugherty, 273 U. S. 135, 71 L. ed. 370.

to legislate—indeed, was treated as inhering in it. Thus there is ample warrant for thinking, as we do, that the constitutional provisions which commit the legislative function to the two houses are intended to include this attribute to the end that the function may be efficiently exercised.

General Purposes of These Investigations.—In general, investigations in pursuance of the law-making function have fulfilled three purposes. First, intricate and deep-rooted questions of public significance, like railroad or corporate combinations in restraint of trade, have been investigated and the findings of these investigations made available for future legislation. Second, occurrences imperilling the public peace and safety, like Burr's conspiracy, have been investigated in view of possible emergency legislation. Finally, growing mostly out of investigations of deep-seated problems, legislation has resulted establishing permanent administrative commissions, like the Interstate Commerce Commission and the Federal Trade Commission. These three types of fact-finding investigations will be considered in the representative cases which will be cited.

Tariff of 1828.—In 1827 the tariff of 1828 was up for debate in the House, and the entire procedure had been marked by bitter partisanship. The demands of Northern protectionists met scathing repudiation from Southern free-traders. Representatives and newspapers were equally as vindictive. No attempt, apparently, was being made to approach the problem as a subject of political economy, or even of sound fiscal expediency. Facts were needed in place of party spleen.

Mallary, Chairman of the House Committee on Manufactures, realized this, and on December 31, 1827, moved a resolution authorizing the committee to send for persons and papers, in order to obtain, if possible, unbiased testimony needed for legislation.[3] Said Edward Livingston in debate:

---

[3] Cong. Deb., 20th Cong., 1st sess., p. 862 (1827). Mallary was a protectionist, a member of the Harrisburg Convention. His committee was composed of five Jackson men and one Adams supporter.

Before I agree to impose this tax upon my constituents, I must be permitted to say I want evidence; that my duty will not permit me to rely on the bare assertion of any one, much less on that of interested persons, be they ever so respectable. . . . A long professional practice has taught me the danger of relying on the testimony of interested witnesses, and has also shown me the great utility of cross examination. From disinterested witnesses it is calculated to elicit truth; but it is invaluable, for the detection of all those subterfuges to which interest resorts, in order to hide truth, or give false color to a true statement.[4]

This motion to clothe a standing committee for the first time with inquisitorial power did not go unchallenged.[5] Nevertheless the majority of the Committee on Manufactures were sustained by a vote of 102 to 88.[6] In the course of the ensuing hearings no less than thirteen New England wool manufacturers and three iron manufacturers were summoned to testify. Considerable light was thrown upon the true condition of the wool industry.[7] It was a surprising thing that the iron men did not ask protection.[8] On January 31, 1828, the committee submitted a bill, which, despite the fears of even its framers lest it should be defeated, became with minor alterations the tariff of 1828.

Conditions in the Southern States, 1871.—In 1871 there was an investigation by a joint committee on conditions in the Southern States. The Fourteenth and Fifteenth Amendments had been passed, and on May 31, 1870, Congress had supplemented attempts to bring order out of chaos by a stringent election law, which was declared unconstitutional five years later.[9] In 1871 the tide of violence and misrule was at a peak point. Complaints from the Southern population against carpet-baggers were being increasingly countered by wild tales, a large proportion of them true, of the high-handed

---

[4] Ibid., p. 872.
[5] Mallary himself did not favor the resolution, but acted only as spokesman of the majority. The general criticism was that the proposal was unheard of, inasmuch as the power had theretofore been employed only by committees acting as judicial bodies (Ibid., p. 882).
[6] Ibid., pp. 868, 888.
[7] F. W. Taussig, Tariff History of the United States, 39-45.
[8] Ibid.
[9] James Schouler, History of the United States, VII, 176.

conduct of the Ku Klux Klan. In fact, the Forty-second Congress, whose first session began March, 1871, was largely occupied in discussing those outrages.

Definite knowledge was needed to supplant or supplement rumors and gossip. By joint resolution of April 7, 1871, a joint committee, with power to send for persons and papers, was instructed " to inquire into the condition of the late insurrectionary states so far as regards the execution of the laws and the safety of the lives and property of the citizens of the United States." [10] Despite considerable objection from the Senators from Georgia and Kentucky, who contended that the proposed investigation was a political move and that it would involve too much expense,[11] the resolution was passed. Seven Senators and nine Representatives finally constituted the committee arising out of the passage of the resolution. The committee reported for the last time March 5, 1872.

Legislation did result in Congress, but it is impossible to say with accuracy just how pertinent to it were the findings of the committee. At any rate, the investigators proceeded to North Carolina, South Carolina, Georgia, Mississippi, and Florida, where scores of witnesses were examined. By Act of February 28, 1871, a second election law with regard to the negro problem was enacted.[12] Almost upon the heels of this, after the investigating committee had been about its duties less than a month, the so-called " Ku-Klux-Act " was passed. This stringent measure, recommended to Congress by an early presidential message, conferred large discretionary powers upon the Executive for the suppression, by military force or otherwise,[13] of all lawless combinations.

An evaluation of the reliability which should be placed upon the vast amount of testimony and report, constituting more than thirteen volumes, is difficult and perhaps not necessary. A large part was recriminating and contradictory. Majority and minority reports became potent campaign ma-

---

[10] Cong. Globe, 42nd Cong., 1st sess., pp. 534-537.
[11] Ibid.
[12] J. F. Rhodes, History of the U. S., VI, 312-313.
[13] Ibid.

terial for the two parties. At any rate, by 1872 the numerous, illegal raids of a brutal nature were brought substantially to an end.[14]

Railway Strike of 1886.—" The year 1886 is likely to be noted as a great strike year," wrote F. W. Taussig in an article composed shortly after the great Southwestern Railroad strike of that year.[15] At least conditions in that section of the country were deemed so critical that the House launched a thorough investigation of the fundamental causes and responsibility for the strike. Owing partly to the depression of 1884, and as the committee concluded, partly to the desire of Jay Gould, owner of the Missouri Pacific system, to increase appreciably its earnings, there had been a general reduction in wages in September, 1884, and again in March, 1885. These cuts were immediately resisted by the shop mechanics in a strike, supported by public opinion, which stopped the freight traffic of the whole Southwestern system. Gould was forced to reëstablish the original wage scale. Encouraged by this victory, when the signal was given on March 6, 1886, for a general walkout, the laborers responded with such unanimity that all wheels came to a standstill. A month later affairs had grown worse instead of better. State militia had been ineffectual. The resulting business slump in Missouri, Arkansas, Kansas, Texas, and Illinois affected the entire commercial life of the country.

With affairs standing at such a pass, Congress deemed it essential to get the true facts of the matter. On April 12, 1886, a resolution was adopted in the House appointing a select committee of seven members to " investigate the cause and extent of the disturbed condition now existing between the railway corporations engaged in carrying on interstate commerce and their employees. . . ." [16] Three days later the committee began its work. Under the resolution creating it

---

[14] Schouler, op. cit., VII, 178.
[15] Southwestern Strike of 1886, Journal of Economics, January, 1887.
[16] 49th Cong., 2d sess., House Rept. No. 4174, p. 1.

the committee was authorized to dispatch committees, send
for persons and papers, and frame "such recommendations
as it may deem proper to make."[17]

The report of the committee consumes two large volumes.
A subcommittee alone traveled 4,880 miles in the strike area
and examined 578 witnesses.[18] The causes and history of the
strike, conduct of the strikers, and actual or estimated economic loss resulting were developed carefully. In attaching
blame to both operators and strikers the committee came to a
decision, since generally concurred in by historians and econo-
mists.[19] The activities of the Knights of Labor in instigat-
ing and conducting the strike were set forth at length, and
the problem of regulating such organizations appeared as an
issue meriting careful and immediate attention. On the
other hand, the use of the black list by corporations was
equally criticised.[20]

In concluding its report the committee stated: " The power
of Congress to deal with the situation presented by this strike
must be found in the provisions of Section 8, Article I, of
the Constitution of the United States, by which Congress is
empowered to provide for the general welfare of the United
States, and to regulate commerce among the several states, and
to establish post-roads." Congress has already provided, by
Section 3964 of the Revised Statutes, "that all railroads or
parts of railroads which are now or may hereafter be in operation shall be post-roads established as such under the authority of the Constitution."

James Buchanan, a member of the investigating committee, felt constrained to write a minority report. He did not
question the constitutionality of the investigation or attack its
findings, but inasmuch as the purpose of the investigation
was presumably to aid legislation it appeared to him that,
" The effect of this late presentation of the report must necessarily be to prevent any consideration of the subject being

---

[17] Ibid.
[18] Ibid., p. 23.
[19] Rhodes, op. cit., VI, 269-279.
[20] 49th Cong., 2d sess., H. Rept. No. 4174, pp. 1-25.

entertained by the present Congress, and the only benefit to
the country at large of the labors of the committee must
consist in the fact that a large mass of testimony covering
every phase of a widely-extended, fiercely-fought, and long-
continued suspension of operations on thousands of miles of
railways has been gathered together for the study of the
economist and the legislator." [21]

The passage of the Interstate Commerce Act, approved
February 4, 1887, apparently brought to fruition Buchanan's
prophecy. This piece of legislation demanded the quality of
information the investigating committee had supplied in
1886. As Cleveland said, " there were abuses and grievances
which demanded correction if they could be so reached that
the remedy would not be worse than the disease." [22]

John Brown's Raid.—The above cases will suffice to demonstrate investigations of deep-rooted public issues. The two
following cases are examples of the manner in which investigations have been used when it was important to discover
rapidly the facts of alarming public occurrences.

Probably the outstanding investigation of this kind, unless
it be the far-reaching Howard investigation of 1856 into the
general disorders in Kansas,[23] was the one occasioned by John
Brown's raid and the seizure of Harper's Ferry in 1859. On
December 14, resolutions were passed by the Senate constituting a special committee of five members, J. M. Mason,
chairman; Jefferson Davis, G. N. Fitch, J. Collamer, and J.
R. Doolittle. The power of sending for persons and papers
was granted the committee in order to determine the character of the armed band, who had supported it, the extent of
monetary endowment from outside sources, the extent of the
damages, and that " said committee report whether any and

---

[21] Ibid., p. 30.

[22] Rhodes, op. cit., VI, 291. For another interesting example
of an investigation under the commerce clause, see the House's
authorization of May 12, 1892, of an inquiry into the employment
of the Pinkerton detectives by companies engaged in interstate commerce (Cong. Rec., 52nd Cong., 1st sess., p. 4222).

[23] 34th Cong., 1st sess., House Rept. No. 200, p. 1.

what legislation may, in their opinion, be necessary on the part of the United States for the future preservation of the peace of the country, or the safety of the public property. . . ." [24]

Many witnesses were summoned and a thorough history of John Brown's career, and of the succor and support he had received from Northern sympathizers were divulged. As to the invasion itself the majority of the committee concluded that " it was simply the act of lawless ruffians, under the sanction of no public or political authority . . . and against which Congress has no power to legislate." Although not advocating definite legislation, the committee earnestly recommended " that provision should be made by the executive, or, if necessary, by law, to keep under adequate military guard the public armories and arsenals of the United States, in some way after the manner now practiced at the navy yards and ports." [25]

New Orleans Riots.—As portentous in content and more fruitful of regulatory legislation was an investigation authorized by the House on December 6, 1866, to inquire into the recent bloody riots in New Orleans. Congress had adjourned on July 28, 1866. Two days later a riot occurred in New Orleans in which were killed thirty-seven negroes, three of their white sympathizers, but only one of the assailants. It was later learned that one hundred and nineteen negroes and seventeen white men had been wounded. Immediate reports badly exaggerated a condition which was deplorable without being exaggerated. The " Radicals " within and without Congress immediately flew into a fever heat. Northern sentiment bitterly assailed the temporizing attitude of President Johnson.

On December 10 the House appointed a " committee of three members . . . whose duties it shall be to proceed to New Orleans . . . to make an investigation into all matters

---

[24] 36th Cong., 1st sess., Sen. Rept. Comm., No. 278, p. 1.
[25] Ibid., p. 19.

connected with the recent bloody riots in that city . . and particularly to inquire into the origin, progress, and termination of the riotous proceedings, the names of the parties engaged in it, the acts of atrocity perpetrated, the number of killed and wounded, the amount and character of the property destroyed, and whether and to what extent those acts were participated in by members of the organization claiming to be the government of Louisiana, and report the facts to the House; and . . . to report such appropriate legislative action as may be required in view of the condition of affairs in the State of Louisiana." [26]

After an exhaustive examination of witnesses on the scene of the disturbance, a majority report signed by two members of the committee was rendered on February 11, 1867. This report covered the instructions of the resolution fully. The meeting of July 30 was termed, " a meeting of quiet citizens, who came together without arms and with intent to discuss questions of public concern." [27] The misfortune was the result of a " purposed attack by the police force of the city upon the convention." [28]

The report concludes with a plea for legislation. " Congress should intervene and should legislate as to secure to the people of Louisiana a republican form of government . . . to the end that Louisiana shall be within the control of loyal men, and not subject to the rule of the same rebel leaders, military and civil, who conducted the war against the government. . . ." [29] The ultimate conclusion reached by the majority was that, " To accomplish that end the condition of affairs in Louisiana requires the temporary establishment of a provisional government." [30]

The answer came in the form of the Reconstruction Act of March 2, passed by the Thirty-ninth Congress over the President's veto. This was followed by the Supplemental

[26] 39th Cong., 2d sess., Cong. Globe, pp. 28, 112.
[27] 39th Cong., 2d sess., H. Rept. No. 16, p. 30.
[28] Ibid., p. 31.
[29] Ibid., pp. 34-35.
[30] Ibid., p. 36.

Reconstruction Act of March 23, again passed over the presidential veto. Finally, an Act of July 19, 1867, was enacted interpreting the above Acts. Of this legislation Rhodes says: "No law so unjust in its policy, so direful in its results, has passed the American Congress since the Kansas-Nebraska Act of 1854." [31]   Southern outrages, largely disclosed by investigation, were the arguments used by "Radicals" in Congress to justify legislation creating five military districts in the South, the registration of voters, and the disenfranchisement of additional white men." [32]

Clayton Act and Federal Trade Commission.—The third result of investigations in pursuance of the law-making function is the establishment of administrative commissions. Permanent administrative agencies have been created to regulate the interests which investigating committees have discovered needed regulating. In other words, these previous investigations, although apparently not resulting in the immediate enactment of legislation, have had a readily recognized cumulative effect. They serve to store up a fund of information on the subject which may be referred to when legislation is being entertained upon a specific measure.

Undoubtedly the best example of such cumulative knowledge, derived from investigation, resulting in regulatory legislation, and the establishment of a commission to carry out the law, is found in the Clayton Act and the establishment of the Federal Trade Commission. [33]   Mr. Joseph E. Davies, the first chairman of the Federal Trade Commission after its organization March 15, 1915, has pointed out the important

---

[31] Rhodes, op. cit., VI, 23.

[32] Ibid. For an interesting investigation of an alleged conspiracy which it was charged jeopardized the public peace and safety, see the report of the Senate committee on "Brewing and Liquor Interests and German and Bolshevik Propaganda," 66th Cong., 1st sess., S. Res. Nos. 307 and 439, S. Doc. No. 62.

[33] This famous investigation was called the "Money Trust Inquiry" (see Cong. Rec., 62nd Cong., 2nd sess., p. 5336, Apr. 22, 1912; also H. R. Res. No. 504). The report was rendered Feb. 28, 1913. The results of the investigation may also be seen in the creation of the Federal Reserve System. This is brought out by H. P. Willis, The Federal Reserve System, 105-115.

part which the findings of congressional investigating committees played in paving the way for the Clayton Act and the establishment of the Federal Trade Commission.[34]

Reference to General Cases.—Space will not permit an extended treatment of additional cases of investigations which serve as an aid to legislation.[35] Other interesting investigations similar to the ones described above have been conducted concerning negro troubles in North Carolina in 1803,[36] the causes of negro immigration northward in 1880,[37] the depression of labor in 1880,[38] the needs of shipping interests in 1882,[39] of the Civil Service in 1882,[40] of express routes in 1888,[41] and of the condition of the Philippine Islands, 1901.[42]

Supplementary Fact-Finding Commissions.—The responsibility of obtaining more and more information of widely

---

[34] Joseph E. Davies, "The Federal Trade Commission," in The Growth of American Administrative Law, 70.

[35] For a comparatively recent investigation which succeeded superlatively in producing the facts of the situation in a very knotty international problem, the case of the investigation of Mexican affairs, in 1919, must be cited. The Senate ordered its committee to discover a vast array of facts: The extent of damages to American citizens resulting from the depredations of bandits; the number killed and wounded; the amount of confiscation of property; the number of citizens in Mexico and the extent of their property holdings; and in general any acts in derogation of the sovereignty of the United States or of the rights of American citizens. Throughout, the committee evinced the highest form of judicial demeanor, and a desire to obtain unbiased facts from anyone who was competent, no matter what his conviction. Two large volumes of testimony were taken. Even missionaries were heard. The findings of the committee are enlightening, and it is difficult to imagine how the committee of foreign affairs could serve with any degree of efficiency whatever without access to an investigative expedient of this character (see 66th Cong., 2nd sess., Senate Res. 106, 163; also Sen. Doc. No. 285).

[36] 7 Ann. Cong., 2nd sess., pp. 386, 534.

[37] 46th Cong., 2nd sess., pp. 19, 3895.

[38] Ibid., pp. 19, 4564, 4576. See also the investigation of Chinese coolie labor in 1876 (Cong. Rec., 44th Cong., 1st sess., p. 4507; 2nd sess., p. 2005).

[39] 48th Cong., 1st sess., p. 7009.

[40] Ibid., p. 86. One of several investigations of the liquor traffic occurred in 1882 (Cong. Rec., 47th Cong., 1st sess., pp. 113, 740).

[41] 50th Cong., 1st sess., p. 16.

[42] 51st Cong., 1st sess., p. 993. The advisability of the Nicaragua route was investigated in 1899 (Cong. Rec., 55th Cong., 3rd sess., p. 360, S. Rep. 1418.

diverse and often highly technical kinds becomes more press-
ing upon Congress each year.   The further Congress enters
into the field of public welfare control, the more complicated
becomes the problem of law-making.   The limits of federal
control over economic and social forces is difficult to foretell.
It is possible that some day the very integrity of our economic life will depend upon the power of Congress to obtain
through its committees or subsidiary fact-finding commissions, the full, complete, continuous access to the facts, for
example, of the water-power industry.

We have seen how Royal Commissions in England have
preëmpted to a large extent this fact-finding function.   To
what extent is such a development possible, or now actually
under way in the United States?

Mr. Daniel E. Lilienthal, in a very able consideration of
this subject, has pointed out that,[43] " Tribunals given only
investigatory or visitorial powers, with no power or duty to
regulate or enforce regulations: simply fact-finding bodies,"
are the Federal Water Power Commission, the United States
Coal Commission, the United States Railroad Labor Board,
the Federal Trade Commission (in some of its activities),
and the United States Tariff Commission.   Although it has
been held by the courts [44] that it does not have power to make
fact-finding investigations where there has been no alleged
violation of law, the Interstate Commerce Commission must
be considered an important indirect contributing factor in
supplementing Congress' fact-finding function.

In addition to these permanent fact-finding commissions,
Congress has of recent years increasingly utilized temporary
commissions, composed largely of technical experts, to investigate and report concerning some specific problem.   Power is
sometimes given such commissions to carry on their investigations longer than the life of one Congress.   Rarely in these
cases has the power to send for persons and papers been

---

[43] D. E. Lilienthal, " The Power of Governmental Agencies to
Compel Testimony," in 39 Harvard Law Review, 694.
[44] Harriman vs. Interstate Commerce Commission, 211 U. S. 407.

granted. They are constitutionally similar and proceed much in the manner of the English Royal Commissions. Outstanding examples of such temporary commissions are the Panama Canal Commission,[45] which gave an exhaustive report to Congress in 1901 upon all phases of the proposed undertaking, the eleven volume report of the Commission on Industrial Relations in 1916,[46] and the Muscle Shoals Commission report of 1925.[47]

We are justified in concluding that owing to the complexity of Congress' law-making function, the unmistakable movement is away from the use of select committees of Congress to make these fact-finding investigations. In their place, permanent administrative commissions are being established, with broad powers of dealing with the problem over which they have legal competence. For special reports concerning problems of a non-permanent nature, commissions of experts, similar to the English Royal Commissions, are being increasingly used. It is to be hoped that eventually Congress will rely almost exclusively upon commissions composed partly of its own members and partly of technical or professional men. The business of the expert is to interpret and instruct, while the function of the legislator is to transmit such information to Congress and to get his recommendations enacted into law. This would mean more thorough reports and greatly increased efficiency in legislation. In Congress, even as in other fields, there must be greater specialization of function.

---

[45] Report of the Panama Canal Commission, 57th Cong., 1st sess., Sen. Doc. No. 54 (1901). This committee was appointed by President Roosevelt. It carried on the investigation for four years.

[46] 64th Cong., 1st sess., S. Doc. No. 19.

[47] 69th Cong., 1st sess., H. Doc. No. 119.

CHAPTER V

The Investigative Power an Instrumentality to Control the Executive Division in Carrying Out the Legislative Will

Necessity for Supervision and Difficulties of Control.—In the first chapter the necessity for Congressional investigations of the executive departments was pointed out. It was shown that the difficulty of control arises from several factors, chief of which is the separation of executive and legislative power, instead of their correlation. It was demonstrated that Congress must obtain information concerning the departments for at least three reasons: first, in order to learn their needs and hence legislate efficiently; second, to make possible alterations in the distribution of work in the respective departments, and finally to determine whether or not the law regulating the work of the departments is being carried out legally, economically, and to best advantage.[1]

One of the constitutional powers of Congress which investigations help to fulfill is the grand jury rôle played by House investigating committees prior to preferring impeachment proceedings. It has been recognized from the first that

---

[1] As John Stuart Mill pointed out, more than sixty years ago, the proper function of a representative assembly is not to administer affairs, but perhaps its most important duty is that of critic and regulator. Mill says, "Instead of the function of governing (i. e. administering), which it is radically unfit for, the proper office of a representative assembly is to watch and control the Government; to throw the light of publicity on its acts; to compel a full exposition and justification of all of them which any one considers questionable; to censure them if found condemnable, and, if the men who compose the government abuse their trust, or fulfill it in a manner which conflicts with the deliberate sense of the nation, to expel them from office, and either expressly or virtually appoint their successors. . . . This is surely ample power, and security enough for the liberty of a nation. . . . Nothing but the restriction of the function of representative bodies within these rational limits will enable the benefits of popular control to be enjoyed in conjunction with the no less important requisites (growing ever more important as human affairs increase in scale and in complexity) of skilled legislation and administration" (J. S. Mill, Essay on Representative Government, 1861).

85

investigations in pursuance of this Constitutional power were unquestionably necessary and proper.   Yet it is a secret to no one, in this country or abroad, that impeachment as a measure of control over civil officers is a very unsatisfactory and wholly insufficient weapon.   It can be called into play only when officers have been charged with very serious offenses.   At best it can only remove from office, instead of preventing abuses of trust.   Then too it is slow, full of evasive loopholes, and so extreme a remedy that even a militant minority party will permit serious infractions before relying upon it as a corrective.

As a matter of fact, most of the abuses which congressional investigating committees inquire into are not even of a remotely impeachable nature.   Their purpose is to discover whether legislative policy is being carried out.   Congressional investigating committees must determine whether the several services are applying their funds for purposes specified, and if so, whether they are spending their apportionment of the appropriation economically, and in such a way as to be most efficient.

Committees on expenditure in both houses of Congress have been generally unsuccessful in seeing that the legislative policy is carried out.   Prior to 1921,[2] Congressional committees of investigation, as imperfect a measure as they are in some respects, had proved themselves the only sure means of obtaining information which officials did not choose to submit voluntarily.   True, there were fairly full reports from all the departments, but it is not at all a remarkable feat for an official to put into his report everything required by law, and at the same time withold much that Congress and its committees would like to know.   The recent Fall, Forbes, and Daugherty cases demonstrate this.

Investigations Where the Principal Question Involved Finances.—In selecting the cases of investigations to be de-

---

[2] In 1921 the Good Budget Bill was passed, creating a Comptroller-General with investigative powers.   This question is discussed below.

scribed in the remainder of the chapter, an attempt has been made to treat separately the several phases of control exercised over the executive departments. These phases have been called investigations, (1) where the principal question involved finances, (2) where impeachment was being considered, (3) where questions of conduct or policy were involved, (4) where presidential elections were inquired into. The four classes make a total of almost two hundred cases.

We shall first consider investigations involving the dispensing of the public funds. In selecting these cases two criteria have been used. First, in authorizing the investigation was it specifically stated in the resolution or agreed upon in debate that the principal object of the investigation was relative to the expenditure of public money? Second, if not specifically avowed, is the subject-matter of the investigation unmistakably of financial character?

General St. Clair.—The first investigation by a Congressional committee of which we have notice was the very interesting inquiry of 1792 into the causes of the failure of the expedition under General St. Clair. This investigation is the first of a group of almost a hundred cases where investigations have been used to control the public finances, particularly their expenditure. The case also marks the first of an astonishingly large number of investigations which have delved into alleged inefficiencies in the Army and Navy departments. It is a remarkable fact that with the exception of the war of 1898,[3] there has been no conflict in which the United States has been engaged where congressional committees did not probe, criticise, and make possible reforms and alterations in the armed forces.

Early in the year 1792 Congress and the country generally learned of the failure of the northwestern expedition under the leadership of General St. Clair. Congress deemed it essential to discover the reasons for the disaster of arms. The

---

[3] President McKinley warded off investigation in this case by appointing the Dodge Commission.

majority everywhere assumed of course that St. Clair was incompetent. On March 27, 1792, after vetoing a resolution authorizing the President to investigate the subject, the House passed a substitute resolution creating a special investigating committee of seven members, with power to send for persons and papers, to inquire and report the circumstances of the defeat.[4]

The power to make the investigation was unanimously assumed, but the question arose as to what basis, or what function, to ascribe to the inquiry. The reply made at this time established once and for all the power of Congress to investigate when considerations involving the public funds can be cited as the necessity of inquiry. On this occasion Mr. Williamson expressed what became the majority view when he stated, " that an inquiry into the expenditure of all public money was the indispensable duty of this House." [5]

Mr. Fitzsimons added that he " was in favor of a committee to inquire relative to such objects as come properly under the cognizance of this House, particularly respecting the expenditure of public money." [6] These answers seem to have stifled effectually an earlier question as to whether such an investigation were advisable when it affected an officer immediately under the control of the President and not impeachable by Congress.[7]

The results of the investigation reveal a truth which has since been repeatedly confirmed, namely, that many times when prior to an investigation it has been generally assumed that personal inefficiency or culpability is to blame for ineffectual expenditure of funds, inquiry shows that such waste is merely the natural concomitant of inefficient organization. This condition has been discovered in practically every branch of the government which congressional committees have investigated. It has been one of the chief means of bringing about alterations in the departments and the introduction of new departments or bureaus.

---

[4] 2 Ann. Cong., pp. 490-494.
[5] Ibid., p. 491.
[6] Ibid., p. 492.
[7] Ibid., p. 491.

In this case the committee unanimously reported it as their sober judgment of General St. Clair that, " the failure can in no respect be imputed to his conduct, either at any time before or during the action; but that as his conduct in all the preparatory arrangements was marked with peculiar ability and zeal, so his conduct during the action furnished strong testimonies of his coolness and intrepidity." [8] The committee's contacts with administrative officials during the investigation, however, convinced them that the real weakness lay in the general plan of the military department, the organization of the army, mismanagement of contracts resulting in delayed and insufficient supplies, " badness of gunpowder," and of inferior supplies generally.[9]

Wolcott, Secretary of Treasury.—The next investigation to be noted is not only an instance of the use of the investigative power to control the manipulation of public funds, but it is also of added interest inasmuch as it is the first of several cases where Cabinet officials have requested an investigation in order to clear their reputations of aspersions or suspicions. On November 24, 1800, the Speaker laid before the House a letter from Wolcott, Secretary of the Treasury, stating that the President had accepted his resignation.   He further stated that inasmuch as suspicions and criticisms had been hurled at his administration of his late office he desired " any investigation which the House of Representatives may be pleased to institute." [10]

On November 25th, 1800, a select committee of seven members was appointed to make the investigation.[11] The power to send for persons and papers was not asked for, it being deemed apparent that the willingness of the Treasury Department to be investigated made it unnecessary. It was noted that such power could later be bestowed if found necessary. The committee's request that the purpose of the investiga-

---

[8] Ibid., p. 1113.
[9] Ibid., pp. 1106-1113.
[10] 6 Ann. Cong., 2nd sess., pp. 786, 979.
[11] Ibid., p. 788.

tion be considered " to examine into the state of the Treasury, the mode of conducting business therein, the expenditures of the public money, and to report such facts and statements as will conduce to a full and satisfactory understanding of the state of the Treasury, since the appointment of the Secretary," was unquestionably adopted.[12]

The report of the committee on January 28, 1801, after a thorough accounting of funds and expenditures, absolved Wolcott of suspicion of maladministration, and concluded that " the Department itself is so devised, as to afford the most perfect security to the nation, from the misapplication of the public moneys." [13]

General Wilkinson.—The next outstanding case of the exercise of the inquisitorial power by Congress in pursuit of its duty as guardian of the public purse occurred in 1810, growing out of charges of alleged conspiracy by General Wilkinson. This investigation probably raised more opposition in Congress than any inquiry before or since. The facts of the case are as follows. On March 21, 1810, Mr. Joseph Pearson of North Carolina, proposed the following resolution in the House: " Resolved, that a committee be appointed to inquire into the conduct of Brigadier Gen. James Wilkinson in relation to his having, at any time, whilst in the service of the United States, corruptly received money from the Government of Spain, or its agents," and to inquire generally into any relationship with foreign agents, or Aaron Burr, and that the results be reported to the House. Power to send for persons and papers was granted.[14]

In the debate on the resolution which began on April 3, 1810, its sponsors stated several grounds of admissability. It was pointed out as a pertinent example that the English

---

[12] Ibid., p. 796. Mr. Griswold very shrewdly observed that, " If it be understood that, on the retirement of every Secretary of the Treasury from office, an inquiry is to be made into his official conduct, it will operate as a general stimulus to the faithful discharge of duty " (Ibid., p. 788).

[13] Ibid., p. 980.

[14] 11 Ann. Cong., 2nd sess., Journal, pp. 306, 339, 343, 346; Annals, pp. 1606, 1727-1757.

House of Commons had inquired into charges that the Duke of York, commander in chief of the army and second son of the King, had speculated in commissions.[15] When the applicability of English precedents was questioned, the argument was rested upon Congress' power over the purse.

" Sir," said Mr. Sheffey, " it is our duty to make this inquiry. The public money is expended on these establishments. The labor of the nation supports them. We extract money from the pockets of the people to appropriate to these purposes, and it is proper to ascertain that those who reap the earnings of the people are worthy of the public confidence." [16] Moreover, he inquired, if the powers of the House were to be strictly circumscribed by the Constitution, how could the investigation of 1801 into the expenses of the previous Administration which had just gone out of office be justified? [17]

As if to resort to all possible justifications for the investigation, its sponsors appealed to the impeaching power. It was true they admitted that under the Constitution no military officer could be impeached. But the President could be. How was the President to be impeached for protecting a corrupt officer until the officer should be proved guilty? [18] Besides, does not Congress have the right to inquire into the condition of the army? If so, does not Congress have the right to inquire into the conduct of individuals comprising it? If not, then the Army belonged to the President, ran the argument, and not to the nation.[19] These arguments seem to have gone home, because the resolution was finally adopted by a vote of 80 to 29.[20]

The committee's report on May first was complete with testimony, but it contained no recommendation. The investigation had been *ex parte*. Once more opposition flared up, and it was contended that the House had assumed the jurisdiction of the courts, and that without question such prejudicial

---

[15] Hinds, III, 83.
[16] 11 Ann. Cong., 2nd sess., p. 1746.
[17] Hinds, III, 83.
[18] Ibid.
[19] Ibid.
[20] Ibid., p. 84.

action would "degrade its legislative character." At the
next session of Congress, on December 18, 1810, the continuation of the inquiry was authorized along with directions to
permit the accused to be heard in his defense.[21] On February 26, 1811, the committee rendered its final report, which
in turn was dispatched to the President for consideration.[22]

Department of War.—Of all administrative departments
the Department of War has come most often under the inquisitorial eye of Congress. This appears nowhere more
plainly than in the period 1815-1820, when congressional
committees investigated the expenses of state militias,[23] alleged defalcations by the Deputy Quartermaster General,[24] the
expenditures of the Army on the northwestern frontier,[25] the
conduct of the Seminole War,[26] illegal executions in the
army,[27] and illegal loans of powder to citizens.[28]

Secretary Calhoun.—Six years later the affairs of the War
Department came sharply to public notice again when Vice-
President Calhoun dispatched a communication to the Speaker
requesting an investigation of his prior administration of
the Department of War.[29] " The conduct of public servants,"
he observed, " is a fair subject of the closest scrutiny and
the freest remarks." [30]   In this case, unlike the Wolcott case,
the House deemed it advisable in ordering the investigation
to clothe the committee with power to send for persons and

---

[21] Ann. Cong., 11th Cong., 3rd sess., pp. 432-450.
[22] Ibid., pp. 1030-1032.
[23] Ann. Cong., 14th Cong., 1st sess., pp. 378, 1047 (1815).
[24] On March 11, 1816, the Speaker laid before the House a
letter from an accountant in the War Department charging Colonel
Thomas with defalcations and misuse of public moneys. On motion
of Mr. McKee a committee was appointed, with power to summon
witnesses and send for necessary documents (Ann. Cong., 14th Cong.,
1st sess., pp. 1199-2000).
[25] This investigation exonerated General Harrison of serious
charges (Ann. Cong., 14th Cong., 2nd sess., 1816, pp. 390, 709).
[26] This case will be considered in the next section under the
supervision of the administration (Ann. Cong., 15th Cong., 2nd sess.,
1818, pp. 37, 256).
[27] Ann. Cong., 16th Cong., 1st sess., I, pp. 727, 2234 (1819).
[28] Ibid., pp. 936, 1791 (1820).
[29] 3 Cong. Deb., p. 574 (1826).
[30] **Ibid.**

papers.[31]   In the report of the committee, rendered February
13, 1827, Calhoun was cleared of all suspicion.[32]   The power
to send for persons and papers appears to have been wisely
granted, judging by the number of subpoenaes dispatched
by the committee.[33]

Defalcations in Customs Service.—It is not to be wondered
at that the customs service, by its nature, should have come in
for its share of investigations.   On January 17, 1839, for
instance, a resolution was adopted in the House which provided that a committee should be appointed, with power to
send for necessary documents and persons, "whose duty it
shall be to inquire into the causes and extent of the late
defalcations of the custom-house at New York and other
places. . . ."[34]   The committee was further instructed to
audit all accounts; determine who the defaulters were; and
the amount, length of time, and causes which led to the
defalcations.

On February 27, 1839, the committee was able to report
various defalcations, attaching blame where it appeared to be
due.   The report stated that serious defalcations at New York
were chiefly attributable to the total lack of competency of
its collector, Swartout.   The report also criticizes "the culpable disregard of the law by the late naval officer at New
York, the First Auditor and Comptroller of the Treasury,
and Swartout's discontinuance of the use of banks as deposi-
tories.[35]   Unqualified blame was attached to the Secretary
of the Treasury for ineffectual supervision, which was considered the root of the evil.[36]

Interior Department.—It is manifestly impossible to consider all governmental agencies with which congressional in-

---

[31] Ibid., p. 576.
[32] Ibid., p. 1123 (1827).
[33] Ibid.
[34] Cong. Globe, 25th Cong., 3rd sess., p. 132 (1839).
[35] 25th Cong., 3rd sess., H. R. Rept. No. 313, Ser. No. 352.
[36] A very successful exposé in relation to custom house investigations was the inquiry into the defalcations of the New York custom-
house.   Wholesale bribery and corruption were revealed (38th Cong.,
2nd sess., H. R. Rept. No. 25).

vestigating committees have dealt. Suffice it to say that between 1792 and 1925 investigating committees have delved, with varying frequency, into every administrative department, excepting the Departments of Commerce and Labor since their separation in 1913, establishing without question of doubt a customary if not a legal claim that the right of appropriation necessitates the power to investigate.[37] It may help to suggest the breadth of this activity to point out that the Departments of Treasury and Interior alone have been investigated approximately fifty times each.

Inquiry in the Interior Department has been especially concerned with the Pension and Patent Offices, and with the Indian Bureau. Investigations of the latter form such a unique commentary upon the effectiveness of investigations that something must be said concerning this brilliant chapter in the story of investigations. The number of investigations is proportionate to the lack of knowledge or the extent of abuse relative to the particular object of investigation. This is preëminently true in regard to the Indian service.

Indian Service.—From 1865-1913 the Indian Bureau was being almost constantly investigated. Between 1865-1900, in many cases it became the practice of the Senate to simply continue its investigating committee on Indian affairs over the recess and into the next session. Among the outstanding results of these investigations are the following. In 1848 a House committee found the Commissioner of Indian Affairs guilty of marked inefficiencies,[38] while in 1853 a Senate committee discovered fraudulent conduct in his office.[39] In 1865

---

[37] Pertinent in this respect is the observation by Mr. Story that, "If there be any general principle which is inherent in the very definition of government, and essential to every step of the progress to be made by that of the United States, it is that every power, vested in a government, is in its nature sovereign, and includes, by force of the term, a right to employ all the means requisite, and fairly applicable to the attainment of the end of such power; unless they are excepted in the Constitution, or are immoral, or are contrary to the essential objects of political society" (Story, Constitutional Limitations, 8th ed., III, 117).

[38] Cong. Globe, 30th Cong., 1st sess., p. 1072; 2nd sess., pp. 242, 252.

[39] Cong. Globe, 32nd Cong., 2nd sess., pp. 381, 1108.

a joint committee recommended the reorganization of the entire department.[40] Alleged frauds in 1872 led to severe censure of the Administration.[41] A joint committee in 1879 recommended the organization of the Indian Bureau as a distinct department of government on a par with other departments.[42]

In the same year a Senate committee discovered serious infringements of treaty stipulations with the Northern Cheyennes.[43] In 1884, 1886, and 1888 congressional committees reported defalcations, maladministration of licensing traders, and of alloting lands.[44] Investigations in 1896, 1898, and 1899 reported fraud in the expenditure of the Osage Indian funds, and abuses in Indian agencies and schools.[45] Senate committees in 1906 and 1910 criticized the administration and alienation of land grants to Indians.[46] Finally, two joint committees in 1913 came to the conclusion, as did preceding committees, that better administrative personnel and not more laws were needed.[47]

Galphin Claim.—The investigation of the Galphin claim by a House committee in 1850 forms another landmark in

---

[40] 39th Cong., 2nd sess., 13 Stat. at L., pp. 572, 573 (1865); Sen. Rep. No. 156, Ser. No. 1279.

[41] Cong. Globe, 42nd Cong., 2nd sess., H. R. Rept. No. 98.

[42] 45th Cong., 3rd sess., Par. 14 Approp. Act, June 18, 1878, 20 Stat. at L., 145, 152, Sen. Rept. No. 693, Ser. No. 1837.

[43] 45th Cong., 3rd sess., Sen. Journal, p. 261, Sen Rep. No. 6701; 46th Cong., 2nd sess., Ser. No. 1898.

[44] Cong. Rec., 48th Cong., 2nd sess., p. 2004; Sen. Repts. Nos. 1392, 1095, 1441, 1552 (1884) Concerning traders, 49th Cong., 2nd sess.; Sen. Rep. No. 2707, Ser. No. 2623 (1886); Respecting lands, Cong. Rec., 50th Cong., 1st sess., pp. 17, 1730, Sen. bill No. 3522 (1888).

[45] 54th Cong., 2nd sess., Sen. Rep. No. 1336, Ser. No. 3475 (1896). Abuses in agencies, Cong. Rec., 55th Cong., 2nd sess., pp. 1495, 4959; Indian schools, Cong. Rec., 56th Cong., 1st sess., pp. 5675, 5934; Sen. Repts. Nos. 60, 895 (1899).

[46] Cong. Rec., 59th Cong., 1st sess., p. 9784 (1906). Sen. Rept. No. 5013; 59th Cong., 2nd sess., Ser. No. 5062 (1907); also Cong. Rec., 61st Cong., 2nd sess., Sen. Res. No. 274; Sen. Repts. Nos. 655, 910 (1910).

[47] 63rd Cong., 3rd sess., Act of June 30, 1913, 38 Stat. at L., 77, 81; Sen. Rept. No. 983, Ser. No. 6762; Act of June 30, 1913, 38 Stat. at L. 77, 100 (1913).

inquiries of this sort. Once more the War Department was involved. On April 3, 1850, the Speaker laid before the House a letter from George W. Crawford, Secretary of War, emulating Wolcott's early example in requesting an investigation of his relationship to the settlement of the Galphin claim.[48] A committee was thereupon appointed, and later, on April 12, it was given the power to send for persons and papers.[49] The committee reported on May 17, condemning the payment of the claim.[50] Immediately a request was made for the House to take steps for the judicial determination of the matter. On September 24 the House Judiciary committee reported a resolution for instituting a suit against Crawford. This recommendation was later adopted by both the House and Senate.[51]

Thomas Ewing, Secretary of Interior.—In the same year the secretary of the Interior was subject to a thorough accounting at the hands of a House investigating committee. The resolution constituting the committee met with heated opposition but finally passed by a vote of 95 to 73.[52] The purpose of the investigation was to determine whether Thomas Ewing, said secretary, had paid certain claims which had not been approved by responsible accounting officers, whether he had misused the appointing power vested in him, and whether he had in his employ certain news correspondents. In its report of September 6, 1850, the committee stated that Ewing was guilty of the first charge, but no remedy was suggested.[53]

Claims and Contracts.—As a rule both houses have been wary about authorizing investigations on the basis of broad or indefinite charges of maladministration of public funds. Not so, however, was an investigation by a Senate committee in 1852, which inquired generally into claims and contracts. The committee was appointed on August 6, 1852, under a reso-

---

[48] Cong. Globe, 31st Cong., 1st sess., p. 628 (1850).
[49] Ibid., p. 719.
[50] Ibid., App. p. 546.
[51] Ibid., pp. 1397, 1934-1937, 1973.
[52] Ibid., pp. 782, 783 (1850).
[53] 31st Cong., 1st sess., H. R. Rept. No. 489, Ser. No. 585.

lution authorizing a select committee to " inquire into abuses, bribery, or fraud, in the prosecution of claims before Congress, commissions, or the Departments, or in passing through Congress bills embracing private, individual, or corporate interests, or in obtaining or granting contracts . . . that said committee have power to send for persons and papers, and examine witnesses on oath." [54]

The committee's activity eventually narrowed down to examining the alleged sale by leading members of the Treasury Department, of contracts for the construction of lighthouses on the Pacific coast, an alleged conspiracy by members in placing contracts for the Capitol extension, and irregularities in the Census Bureau. The report concluded that certain officials in the public employ had been dishonest. Outside of criticising the existing arrangement for dispensing public funds it contained no concrete suggestions. [55]

Alaska Purchase Scandal.—No sooner had the final signatures been appended to the document for the purchase of Alaska than stories of wholesale bribery in aiding the passage of the bill began to circulate. It was said that the President had been guilty of " a high-handed usurpation." One newspaper charged that of $7,200,000 voted to pay for Russia's colonies in America only $5,000,000 had reached the government. [56] It was alleged that the remainder had been distributed among members of Congress, newspaper men, lobbyists, and government officials, to secure the bill's passage in Congress.

The Committee on Public Expenditures was given power to send for persons and papers in making the investigation. [57] Secretary Seward, Riggs, the Washington Banker, through whom the money passed on its way to the Russian legation, Spinner, the Treasurer of the United States, Robert J. Walker, who had been retained by the Russian Legation for

---

[54] Cong. Globe, 32nd Cong., 1st sess., p. 2100 (1850).

[55] Specl. sess. of 1853, Sen. Rept. No. 1, Ser. No. 688.

[56] Oberholtzer, A History of the United States since the Civil War, I, 555.

[57] Cong. Globe, 40th Cong., 2nd sess., p. 4394.

the purpose of influencing legislation, and several others appeared for examination.

The committee made two reports. It appeared that Mr. Walker had received $26,000 in gold and that he had given $5,000 in greenbacks, taken from this sum, to counsel associated with him in the case. It was also learned that $3,000 had been offered to a certain newspaper man for "valuable service by opening its columns" to articles favorable to the purchase. Charges of the complicity of members of Congress, or of the government, were not established. Four members of the committee contented themselves by denouncing "the loose morality" of several Washington journalists who sent to their papers "nebulous gossip" instead of facts.[58]

Investigations where Impeachment Was Being Considered. —The instances we have cited of investigations pertaining to the public finances only begin to demonstrate the ambit of Congress' activity in this respect. Investigations have unquestionably saved the people thousands of dollars outright, and a great deal more by exposing incompetent or dishonest management of funds.

This record of achievement is rivalled by the accomplishments of investigations in relation to impeachment proceedings. Their number is much fewer. There is much in favor of maintaining that congressional investigating committees are as essential to impeachment as a grand jury investigation is to a criminal trial. The power of making such investigations has been asserted from the first, and the power has never been judicially questioned.

Daniel Webster, Secretary of State.—Of outstanding interest among inquiries conducted by House committees to determine if, in the alleged misconduct of officers of the executive and judicial departments, there were grounds for impeachment, stands the case of an investigation of the official conduct of Daniel Webster, Secretary of State. On April 9, 1846, C. J. Ingersoll arose in the House and stated that

---

[58] 40th Cong., 3rd sess., H. R. Rept. No. 35.

he had information relative to the Secretary of State which, if substantiated, would be grounds for preferring impeachment charges. He continued by saying he had reference to the misappropriation of the secret fund appropriated for the State Department in negotiating upon the northeastern boundary question.[59] The dispensation of this sum had been accorded by law to the President's sole discretion, whereas, it was charged, Webster had spent the money without consulting the President.

The action of the House on April 27, in response to the charges of Ingersoll, seemed aimed to inculpate the accuser and neglect the accused. Mr. Schenck, of Ohio, unexpectedly moved a resolution appointing an investigating committee to inquire, "how the seal of confidence imposed by law, heretofore uniformly preserved in relation to the expenditure of said secret fund, has come to be broken." [60] The same day, however, the above resolution was amended to create another committee, " to inquire into the truth of the charges this day made in this House by Mr. C. J. Ingersoll against Mr. Daniel Webster, with a view to founding an impeachment against said Daniel Webster; and that said committee have power to send for persons and papers, books and vouchers." [61]

The committee's report on June 9, 1846 stated that many witnesses had been examined, among them Mr. Tyler, late President of the United States. Tyler had stated that during his Presidency secret funds had been independently dispensed by the Secretary of State, whom he considered the fittest person, and such, he said, was the proper course according to law and usage in Mr. Webster's case.[62] In this conclusion the committee concurred. The apparent shortage in the balance of the fund was attributed to Mr. Webster's inability to obtain certain vouchers. Inasmuch as important political secrets had been uncovered during the investigation the committee advised sealing up the evidence and depositing it in

---

[59] Cong. Globe, 29th Cong., 1st sess., p. 636.
[60] Ibid., p. 734.
[61] Ibid., p. 735.
[62] Ibid., p. 946.

safe keeping. The conclusion was that " there is no proof
in relation to any of the charges to impeach Mr. Webster's
integrity, or the purity of his motives in the discharge of the
duties of his office." [63]

President Andrew Johnson.—The part played by the investigating committee in the prelude to the impeachment and
trial of Andrew Johnson is a matter of such common record
that the investigation need only be mentioned here. When
the inquiry finally was authorized on January 6, 1867, impeachment had been impending, under the pressure of radical
influence, for more than a year. The committee was authorized to inquire into the official conduct of Andrew Johnson
and report whether in their opinion he had been guilty of
" other high crimes and misdemeanors," which, in addition
to treason and bribery, were impeachable offences under the
Constitution.[64]   Near the end of the session the committee reported that enough evidence had been found to warrant the
continuation of the investigation.[65]   Accordingly, when the
Fortieth Congress convened on March 4, 1867, the Judiciary
committee was again intrusted with the taking of testimony.[66]

Mr. Ashley, who moved the original resolution, hoped the
committee would discover grounds for impeachment upon two
counts, to wit, the connivance of President Johnson in the
assasination of Lincoln, and proof that the President had
used the pardoning power improperly and corruptly. However, on June 1, 1867, the committee by a vote of five to four
came to the conclusion that there was no ground for impeachment. However, under pressure of a militant minority, hearings were reopened. Finally, after the President's suspension of Stanton and the removal of Sheridan, one member
of the nine shifted ground, and on November 25 a majority
of the committee reported in favor of impeachment charges.
An able minority report, signed by two Republicans and two

---

[63] Ibid.
[64] Rhodes, op. cit., VI, 98.
[65] 39th Cong., 2nd sess., House Rept. No. 7, Ser. 1417.
[66] Ibid.

Democrats, was accepted by the House instead, and on December 7 the House rejected impeachment by a vote of 108 to 57.[67] Impeachment was finally agreed to on February 24th 1868.

Cases Cited.—Other notable investigations in aid of the impeaching process are found in the cases of General Clark in 1798; [68] Justice Samuel Chase, 1804; [69] Judge John Pickering, 1803; [70] Judge W. H. Humphreys, of Tennessee, in 1862; [71] Secretary of War Belknap, 1876; [72] and Judge English, in 1925.[73]

Investigations where Questions of Conduct or Policy Were Involved.—Investigations of the Administration and the Executive where questions of conduct or policy were involved constitute a class which in number and importance are unsurpassed by any group mentioned so far. These investigations have succeeded in accomplishing a variety of things, such as placing responsibility for malfeasance or non-feasance, or of limiting administrative attempts to exercise a margin of discretionary power. All such investigations have in some measure increased the knowledge of Congress and made wiser legislation possible. Many of them have been fruitful of laws reorganizing or redistributing the administrative departments. The Chief Executives themselves have not escaped. Indeed the President and his Cabinet have been subjected to investigation twenty-three times, beginning with John Adams and ending with Woodrow Wilson.[74]

The House very early overruled the objection that inquiry into the conduct of government clerks would be an infringe-

---

[67] Cong. Rec., 40th Cong., 1st sess., pp. 1087, 1402. An interesting account of the investigation and trial is found in Rhodes, VI, 98-157. See also Dewitt, Impeachment and trial of A. Johnson.

[68] 5 Ann. Cong., I, p. 962; II, p. 1559.

[69] 8 Ann. Cong., 1st sess., pp. 806, 1124.

[70] Ibid., pp. 380, 1097.

[71] 37th Cong., 2nd sess., Cong. Rec., pp. 1991, 2039.

[72] Smith, Digest of Precedents, 53rd Cong., 2nd sess., Sen. Misc. Doc., XII, pp. 553-567.

[73] Cong. Rec., 68th Cong., 2nd sess., p. 2536, H. Rep. No. 1638.

[74] Galloway, "Investigative Function of Congress," Amer. Pol. Sci. Rev. XXI, No. 1, p. 47.

ment on the executive power. On January 16, 1818, Mr. John Holmes of Massachusetts, proposed a resolution for a committee " to inquire whether any and what clerks or other officers in either of the Departments, or in any office at the seat of the General Government, have conducted themselves improperly in their official duties; and that the committee have power to send for persons and papers." [75] Broad as the terms of this resolution were it passed the House by a large majority, with very little debate.[76] As the result of the committee's investigation and report a second committee was appointed with instructions to frame a bill more definitely allocating duties and centering responsibility in the departments.[77]

General Jackson and the Seminole War.—The same year reveals an investigation into the conduct of General Jackson during the Seminole War. This inquiry had an immediate significance, and it also undoubtedly colored Jackson's attitude toward congressional investigations when he became President. It is also of interest because it marks the first time the Senate bestowed upon an investigating committee the power to send for persons and papers. The resolution adopted December 18, 1818, read as follows:

That the Message of the President, and documents relative to the Seminole War, be referred to a select committee, who shall have authority, if necessary, to send for persons and papers: that said committee inquire relative to the advance of the United States troops into West Florida; whether the officers in command at Pensacola and St. Marks were amenable to, and under the control of Spain; and, particularly, what circumstances existed, to authorize or justify the commanding general in taking possession of those posts.[78]

On February 24, 1819, the committee members reported that, " they have under the authority conferred upon them, called for and examined persons and papers." The testimony revealed that General Jackson had conducted his troops

---

[75] Ann. Cong., 15th Cong., 1st sess., p. 783.
[76] Ibid., p. 786.
[77] Ibid., p. 1649.
[78] Ann. Cong., 15th Cong., 2nd sess., pp. 37, 256.

very much in his customary independent fashion, and that certain restrictions of the Constitution in regard to due authorization did not bear at all heavily upon his conscience. Consequently the committee concluded its report with unminced censure of Jackson's usurpation of power. It made no specific recommendations.[79]

Edwards-Crawford Dispute.—In 1824 inquiry to supervise the administrative and executive departments appeared in an unusual rôle growing out of a quarrel between two officers of the government, Ninian Edwards, minister to Mexico, and W. H. Crawford, Secretary of the Treasury. On April 19, 1824, the Speaker submitted to the House certain addresses of Ninian Edwards, late Senator from Illinois and Minister to Mexico, in which Edwards presumed to absolve himself from certain adverse criticism growing out of correspondence of the Secretary of the Treasury to Congress, relative to the deposits of public money in state banks.

Edwards, it seems, had retaliated by accusing Crawford of illegal deposits and expenditures of money, and the supression of papers and documents which should have been communicated under resolutions to that effect by Congress. Mr. Daniel Webster, of Massachusetts, immediately suggested that the public session of the House was not a fitting place to air the contests of public men. Consequently on April 20 an investigating committee was appointed, with power to send for persons and papers in examining the charges made by Edwards.[80] By a resolution of April 22 the committee was authorized to request Edwards to be present during the hear-

---

[79] 15th Cong., 2nd sess., S. Rept. No. 100, Ser. No. 15. The following year the House, deciding that Jackson had misapplied certain funds, in raising troops without congressional sanction, appointed a committee to investigate his conduct of the Seminole War from this angle (Ann. Cong., 16th Cong. 1st sess., p. 717). Although the committee concluded that the alleged charges were true, it suggested no action inasmuch as "the faithful discharge of the duties of the several committees of the House furnished an adequate remedy . . ." (16th Cong., 1st sess., H. R. Rept. No. 72, Ser. No. 40, p. 12.)

[80] Ann. Cong., 18th Cong., 1st sess., p. 2431.

ings, and to apprise President Monroe of the action of the House.

In the hearings that followed Edwards was heard under oath. Senators Benton, of Missouri, and Noble, of Indiana, besides several members of the House, were called to testify. Crawford, although not appearing personally, was represented by attorney and also by a representative of the department. On May 25 the committee made its preliminary report. By resolution of the same day it was ordered to continue the investigation during the recess of the House. The committee finally reported that nothing had appeared out of the testimony to in any way impeach the integrity of the Secretary, but beyond that point they were content with presenting the facts and the testimony.[81] Edwards' resignation was received the same year.

Post Office Department.—In 1830 the Post Office Department, which had already been the subject of investigations in 1820 and 1822, came again under the inquiring eye of Congress. By resolution of December 15, 1830, a Senate committee was ordered:

> To examine and report the present condition of the Post Office Department; in what manner the laws regulating that department are administered; the distribution of labor; the number of clerks; and the duty assigned to each; the number of agents, where and how employed; the compensation of contractors; and, generally, the entire management of the department; and whether further, and what, legal provisions may be necessary to secure the proper administration of its affairs.[82]

By resolution of January 27, 1831, the Senate gave the committee power to send for persons and papers.[83] Strangely enough it soon became evident that the chief aim of the investigation was to delve into the reasons for various dismissals in the department. Believing that the Senate had no right to inquire into the President's reasons for making removals, Livingston accordingly amended a motion of February 2, 1831, to read that " inquiry into the reasons which

---

[81] Ibid., p. 2770.
[82] 7 Cong. Deb., p. 4.
[83] Ibid., p. 40.

have induced the Postmaster General to make any removals
of his deputies are not meant to be within the purview of this
investigation." This resolution was adopted by the narrow
margin of 24 to 21.[84] The committee's report on March 3,
1831, catalogued faithfully all the information requested in
authorizing the investigation, and suggested that amendatory
legislation was needed.[85]

President and Cabinet.—Two years later the House launched a sweeping inquiry into charges against the President and
his Cabinet, authorizing a committee to determine, " whether
an attempt was made by the late Secretary of War, John
H. Eaton, fraudulently to give to Samuel Houston, a contract . . . and that said committee be further instructed to
inquire whether the President of the United States had any
knowledge of such attempted fraud, and whether he disap-
proved of the same; and that the committee have power to
send for persons and papers." [86] Despite the breadth of the
resolution, the committee early discovered that' the charges
were groundless. Accordingly their report absolved Eaton
of all corrupt charges, without the necessity of seriously
impugning the motives or actions of the President and other
members of his Cabinet.[87]

President Jackson's Administration.—In the same year,[88]
and again in 1854,[89] the House levelled its inquisitorial power

---

[84] Ibid., pp. 194-197, 208.
[85] 21st Cong., 2nd sess., S. Doc., No. 73, Ser. No. 204.
[86] Cong. Deb., 22nd Cong., 1st sess., pp. 3022, 3261.
[87] 22nd Cong., 1st sess., H. R. Rept. No. 502, Ser. No. 228.
[88] 22nd Cong., 1st sess., H. R. Rept. No. 283. Ser. No. 225,
Reappointed: 8 Cong. Deb., p. 1846 (1832); 22nd Cong., 1st sess.,
H. R. Rept. No. 460, Ser. No. 227; Landis, op. cit., pp. 179-181.
[89] The resolution of Polk was as follows: " That a select committee be appointed for the purpose of ascertaining, as far as
practicable, the cause of the commercial embarrassment and distress
complained of by numerous citizens of the United States . . . of
inquiring whether the charter of the Bank of the United States has
been violated, and also what corruptions and abuses have existed in
its management; whether it has used its corporate power of money
to control the press to interfere in politics, or influence elections,
and whether it has any agency through its management or money,
in producing the existing pressure." 10 Cong. Deb., pp. 2370,

into the affairs and administration of the Bank of the United States. The same decade brings to focus the outspoken opposition of President Jackson to investigations of himself and his subordinates. On December 31, 1836, Mr. Henry A. Wise, of Virginia, one of the most persistent critics of executive patronage, succeeded in getting a resolution past the House authorizing a committee with power to send for persons and papers to investigate the condition of the executive departments in regard to their integrity and efficiency.[90] The resolution passed by a vote of 165 to 9.

The first action of the committee was to send resolutions to the President and the departments requesting them to advise the committee of all appointments made and salaries paid without the advice and consent of the Senate.[91] In addition the aforesaid were to report all those who " received salaries without being in office." [92] The prejudicial tone of the communication brought from President Jackson the following retort, " I shall on the one hand cause every possible facility consistent with law and justice to be given to the investigation of specific charges; and, on the other, shall repudiate all attempts to invade the just rights of the Executive departments and of the individuals composing the same." [93]

It must be admitted that the terms of the investigation were decidedly general, and that the committee was either purposely or unwittingly tactless. However, despite constantly growing antagonism by the President, the committee, chiefly because of the zeal of Wise, its chairman, was able to elicit testimony in the departments for a further period of two months. General questions were asked concerning the

---

3476 (1834). In this and the investigation of 1832 John Quincy Adams appeared as the " first ardent opponent " of unlimited investigation. Eventually fourteen directors of the bank who had been subpoenaed refused to testify, and the inquiry was allowed to die a natural death (Landis, op. cit., 181).

[90] Cong. Deb., 24th Cong., 1st sess., p. 1057.
[91] 24th Cong., 2nd sess., H. R. Rept. No. 194, p. 4.
[92] Ibid., p. 5.
[93] Ibid., p. 19.

Treasury Department,[94] General Land Office, Secretary of State, Secretary of War, and the Paymaster Generals of the same. The testimony appeared to point unmistakably to fraud by Joseph W. Reckless, collector of customs at Perth Amboy, New Jersey.

In reporting on March 3, 1837, however, the majority of the committee was forced to admit that the investigation could not, indeed should not, be completed.[95] Wise stood firm to the end, and in a minority report denied that the terms of the investigation were excessive, defending the "general" investigative power of Congress and particularly of his committee.[96]

Deposit Banks.—The same year reveals a colorful inquiry by the same session of the House, to determine whether certain banks of deposit had agents in Washington to transact business with the Treasury Department, and whether such agents received any compensation from the Treasury Department.[97] The committee appointed January 3, 1837, was given power to send for persons and papers. Testimony pointed an accusing finger toward Reuben W. Whitney, who had tried the patience of the House to breaking as a contumacious witness in the investigation of the executive departments, noted above.[98]

On March 1, 1837, the committee concluded that "the several banks employed for the deposit of public money have

---

[94] In the course of the investigation, Woodberry Levi, Secretary of the Treasury, was asked, "Do you know whether any officer of the Treasury Department or of any of either of the Executive Departments, has been concerned, individually or in a company with others, in purchasing or speculating in public lands? Has the President and others established presses in Washington and elsewhere to promote the election of Martin Van Buren?" (ibid., pp. 80, 81).

[95] "This investigation could be instituted only for one of two purposes . . . impeachment or legislation; they have shown it was not for legislation, because no defect in the laws has been anywhere alleged, only in their execution. . . . It was not the laws, therefore, that the resolution proposed to reform, but the administration of those laws" (ibid., p. 5).

[96] Ibid., p. 5.

[97] Cong. Deb., 24th Cong., 1st sess., pp. 1225-1226 (1837).

[98] Hinds, op. cit., III, 2-8.

not all, or any of them, by joint or several contract, employed an agent to reside at the seat of government . . . but that it is clearly shown that, in particular instances, some of the deposit banks have transacted business of an important character with the Treasury Department through their agent, Reuben M. Whitney." [99]

Captain J. D. Elliott, U. S. N.—In 1839 the House demonstrated that it was just as concerned with the conduct of navy officials as with the administration of the army, by appointing a committee to investigate charges against J. D. Elliott of the Mediterranean squadron. The object of the inquiry was set out in the resolution as " inquiry into the official conduct of Captain Jesse D. Elliott, of the United States navy, while in command of the squadron in the Mediterranean . . . and particularly into allegations of tyranny and oppression toward officers under his command. . . ." [100]

Party Patronage under Polk.—In 1850 the President again came in for investigation when the House appointed a committee to inquire into the political activities of federal office holders. By resolution of May 6, 1850, the committee was instructed to discover what officers or clerks under the late Polk administration had written for newspapers; their salaries for such activity; whether any of the officials of the last administration had absented themselves from duty because of political pursuits; and whether a compulsory levy had been made on all office-holders to secure the election of Polk in his contest with General Taylor.[101]

Under power granted them to send for persons and papers the committee took a great deal of testimony among officers and clerks in the departments. The committee's report on September 30 revealed that two clerks in the Post Office Department had admitted being regular party correspondents,

---

[99] 24th Cong., 2nd sess., H. R. Rept. No. 193, Ser. No. 305, p. 2.
[100] Cong. Globe, 25th Cong., 3rd sess., p. 195. Power to send for persons and papers was granted. No definite action resulted other than sending the report to the proper executive officers.
[101] Ibid., 31st Cong., 1st sess., p. 818.

and that several others in various departments had admitted being party correspondents from time to time. Practically no department had escaped the campaign levy, and even the state organizations had been systematically worked for subscriptions. The report closes with three resolutions denouncing the present system of party patronage and political levy, asserting that office holders should not be permitted to "attempt to influence the votes of others, or take any part in the business of electioneering." [102] That such a condition was allowed to flourish was attributed to the connivance of the President.

Covode Investigation.—The Covode investigation, growing out of charges against President Buchanan and his cabinet, probably holds first eminence among investigations of the executive. On March 5, 1860, the House adopted a resolution by Mr. John Covode which provided for a committee to "investigate whether the President of the United States or any other officer of the government has, by money, patronage, or other and improper means, sought to influence the action of Congress, or any committee thereof, for or against the passage of any bill pertaining to the rights of any State or Territory, and whether any officer or officers of the government have, by combination or otherwise, prevented or defeated, or attempted to prevent and defeat, the execution of any law now upon the statute book, and whether the President has failed or refused to compel the execution of any law thereof. . . ." [103]

Not unlike President Jackson, President Buchanan saw fit to submit his solemn protest against the appointing of such a committee.[104] This time, however, the answer of the committee was short and decisive. Quoting the words of a committee appointed in 1826, they replied: " The power of patronage, unless checked by the vigorous interposition of Congress, must go on increasing until federal influence in

---

[102] Ibid., 31st Cong., 1st sess., Appendix, pp. 1319-1322.
[103] Ibid., 36th Cong., 1st sess., p. 997.
[104] 36th Cong., 1st sess., H. R. Rept. No. 648, p. 2.

many parts of this confederation will predominate in elections as completely as British influence predominates in the elections of Scotland and Ireland, in rotten-borough towns, and the great naval stations of Portsmouth and Plymouth." [105]

Inspired by Covode, the committee summoned eighty witnesses and investigated four principal subjects. They submitted a voluminous record. Their report of June 16, 1860, presents charges which would appear grave enough to justify proffering impeachment charges. [106] In regard to the passage of the Lecompton Constitution the report states that the President was guilty of an " attempt to convert Kansas into a slave state by means of forgeries, fraud, and force." That he had used the " open employment of money in the passage of the Lecompton bill in Congress." Furthermore, ran the indictment, the President had made an offer " to purchase newspapers and newspaper editors." " Proscription of Democrats of high standing who would not support the Lecompton and English bills," it was said, " was grossly resorted to by the unscrupulous President." [107]

In attempting to explain the causes of abuses at the Philadelphia custom house and other public buildings, the committee submitted that " this persistent violation of law is only surpassed by the meanness of such an act. The inference is obvious, viz: to retain the patronage." [108] With reference to public printing it was stated that, " the excess beyond a fair price has been, with the knowledge and consent, if not by the direct order, of the President, squandered upon a profligate press devoted to the interest of the Administration." Party assessment for political purposes was proved conclusively, and the committee concluded in this respect that " when money is used for the purpose of corrupting the freedom of elections, of buying votes, and maintaining a force to overcome the timid . . . more especially when this

---

[105] Ibid.
[106] Ibid.
[107] Ibid., p. 6.
[108] Ibid., p. 9.

is done by officers of the government, the evil becomes one requiring the most careful investigation." [109]

Committee on Conduct of Civil War.—Of almost equal reputation, and undoubtedly more constructive in its results, was an investigation authorized in 1861 to inquire into the disasters of Bull Run and Edward's Ferry.[110] Southern victories had not only moderated the easy optimism of the North, but had left Congress and the Northerners badly bewildered. Perhaps, it was thought, the President was to blame. Certainly there was something wrong with the War Department. At any rate, Congress was determined to dis-- cover where the source of weakness lay, and the investigating committee appeared as the most efficient device. In the crisis Congress apparently did not trouble itself with the reflection that inasmuch as the President is the commander-in-chief of the Army, such interference constituted a serious infringement of the executive prerogative. In the Senate the resolution passed by a vote of 33 to 3, and in the House there was not even debate or division.[111]

This investigation marks the use for the first time of the joint investigating committee. As amended and finally adopted the resolution was made to permit a committee " to inquire into the conduct of the present war, and that they have power to send for persons and papers, and to sit during the sessions of either House of Congress." [112]

The Wade committee, so constituted, went about its duties

[109] Ibid., pp. 22-29. Mr. Warren Winslow wrote an able minority report in which he stated that the investigation had been " an opportunity and temptation to reckless and malignant men to revenge their disappointment by calumnious imputations against officers of the government." There was unquestionably much justification for his remark. Historians are generally agreed that the damaging disclosures of this investigation contributed a great deal to the election of Lincoln (see Schouler's History of the United States, V. 450-452).

[110] Cong. Globe, 37th Cong., 2nd sess., p. 16.

[111] Ibid., pp. 32, 40. Senator Fessenden probably did not exaggerate when he said in debate, " We must satisfy the people of this country that things are going well, or we shall find ourselves in a condition very soon when they will not go at all " (ibid., p. 31).

[112] Ibid., p. 32.

vigilantly during the entire course of the war. Their reports comprise four large volumes.[113]   In truth it may be said that this committee took over a partial control of Union operations. Practically no phase of the conflict escaped the inquisitorial eye.   Battles, disloyal employees, naval stations, surrenders at sea, military and naval supplies, were summarily investigated.   War contracts were inspected with special zeal.   If legislative meddling could be shown to be damaging from a strategic standpoint, at least Congress was able to legislate with adequate knowledge and to hold the officials in Washington and upon the line of battle to strict accountability.

Many Investigations during Grant Administration.—Since the Civil War, investigations of the executive have been as numerous as in the early period, with, if anything, more meticulous regard on the part of Congress for details.   During Grant's eight turbulent years investigating activity reached its high water mark.   Between 1869 and 1877 there were upwards of thirty-five investigations aimed at controlling expenditures and supervising the administration.   In 1884 occurred the famous investigation of the Star Route scandals.[114]   During the next two decades, when the struggle for civil service reform held the center of the political stage, congressional investigations contributed largely toward discovering the true state of conditions.

Civil Service.—The civil service investigation of 1886 may be taken as an example.   On March 13 of that year the Senate, in pursuance of an act of January 16, 1883, to regulate and improve the civil service, appointed a committee to determine the truth of certain alleged abuses in the system.[115]

---

[113] 38th Cong., 2nd sess., S. Rept. No. 142, Ser. No. 1241-1242 (Supplement).

[114] This scandal, which involved many prominent men, arose concerning the fraudulent manipulation of contracts to transport United States mail (Cong. Rec., 48th Cong., 1st sess., p. 1982; H. Ex. Doc. No. 100.).

[115] Cong. Rec., 50th Cong., 1st sess., p. 1904.   McConachie states that in 1866 the joint Committee on Retrenchment arose and ran its course of six years, laying bare abuses in the disordered civil

Just prior to this President Cleveland had vigorously warned subordinates in the departments against political patronage, unseemly partisan activities, and a general recurrence of the spoils system.[116] The committee's report of October 10, 1888, disclosed that inquiry in the several departments, and in the States of Pennsylvania, Maryland, Indiana, and New York showed the recurring prevalence of just the abuses the President had counselled against.

The report charges that " partisan changes have been made . . . in a wholesale way under no pretense that the good of the public service demanded it." [117] Federal officials, it was said, use their positions as centers for political propaganda and activity. Finally, ran the charge, " the system of levying tolls and assessments upon federal office-holders for political purposes has continued without interruption since the administration came into place." [118] The committee concluded moreover that " in no case does the committee find any Federal officer has been disciplined or punished for such interference in politics, but on the other hand such interference has been repeatedly recognized and rewarded.[119]

Administrative Commissions.—The establishment of additional bureaus and boards by Congress during the past score of years has been of great utility, for reasons cited above. Nevertheless, they too necessitate investigations, at intervals, because only in this way can Congress supervise their efficiency and activity. For instance, in the past half dozen years Congress has investigated the United States Shipping Board (1920),[120] the Federal Trade Commission (1919),[121] the

---

service, and that historically it stands in a parental relation to the present standing committees on Civil Service and Retrenchment in the Senate, and on Civil Service Reform in the House (Congressional Committees, 233).

[116] 50th Cong., 1st sess., S. Rept. No. 2373, p. 1.
[117] Ibid., p. 46.
[118] Ibid., p. 47.
[119] Ibid.
[120] Cong. Rec., 56th Cong., 3rd sess., H. R. Rept. No. 1399.
[121] Ibid., 66th Cong., 1st sess., S. Res. No. 295.

Vocational Education Board (1920),[122] the War Finance Corporation (1923),[123] the Veterans' Bureau (1924),[124] the Shipping Board (1924),[125] and the Tariff Commission (1926).[126]

Investigations where Presidential Elections Were Inquired into.—A third group of investigations, few in number, remain to be mentioned under our classification suggested above. They are those inquiries, notably between 1875-1877, which have been ordered by Congress in the case of the presidential election being thrown upon Congress for decision. Another phase of this investigative activity is inquiry of illegal expenditure by presidential candidates.

Hayes-Tilden Dispute.—The pretensions of this chapter will permit little more than mention of these investigations, the details of which are amply recorded in history. The investigating committees appointed by the House in 1875 to determine the issue between Hayes and Tilden visited Florida, Mississippi, and Louisiana, the principal seats of the dispute; and also South Carolina and certain Northern cities where there had been violence.[127] The reports of these committees paved the way for the inauguration of Hayes.[128]

Elections of 1920.—A more recent example of investigative activity respecting presidential elections is found in the Senate inquiry of the campaign expenditures in the election of 1920. Senator Borah was chairman of the committee, vested with power to send for persons and papers. His committee in-

---

[122] Ibid., 66th Cong., 2nd sess., H. Res. No. 495; H. R. Rept. No. 1102.
[123] Ibid., 68th Cong., 1st sess., S. Rept. No. 1, p. 69.
[124] Ibid., 68th Cong., 1st sess., S. Rept. No. 103, pt. 2.
[125] Ibid., p. 3731.
[126] Ibid., 69th Cong., 1st sess., pp. 5444, 2636.
[127] Ibid., 44th Cong., 2nd sess.. H. R. Rept. No. 140.
[128] Rhodes, op. cit., VII, 277-279. "On May 17, 1877, the Democratic House passed a resolution for the appointment of the committee to investigate Hayes' title and aroused some alarm lest an effort might be made to oust President Hayes and inaugurate Tilden. Although this alarm was stilled less than a month later by a decisive vote of the House, the action and investigation were somewhat disquieting" (Ibid., VIII, 101).

quired fully into the expenditures of the candidates of both major parities.[129] Largely as a result of the investigation's revelations, the same session of Congress passed a bill more carefully regulating the publicity of campaign funds.[130]

Credit Mobilier Investigation Served Two Functions.—It would be contrary to the writer's desire if one should gain the impression from the foregoing that the suggested classification is rigid, or that it precludes the possibility of justifiably considering certain investigations under other or several of the suggested captions. That such treatment is possible and at times highly desirable may be shown by briefly referring to the sensational Credit Mobilier investigation of 1872-1873. This investigation, conducted by two distinct committees of the House and a third of the Senate, might be considered in connection with the investigations whose purpose it is to inquire into the conduct of members of Congress, or as an inquiry into the alleged conspiracy of the administration. Two additional objects might reasonably be attached to the investigation, namely those of obtaining information for legislation and of inquiring into the expenditure of public money.

The history of the case may be stated briefly. Soon after the opening of the session of the House in December, 1872, the Speaker, James G. Blaine, whose name had been bandied about in connection with the Union Pacific scandal, called S. S. Cox to the chair and moved the appointment of a committee to determine whether any member had been bribed by the Ames' interests.[131] A few weeks later a second committee was appointed to determine whether the government had been defrauded, because of possible conspiracy in high places, by the Credit Mobilier.[132] These two committees proceeded with their work simultaneously. Meanwhile the Senate had also

---

[129] Cong. Rec., 66th Cong., 2nd sess., Sen. Res. No. 357.
[130] 66th Cong., 2nd sess., p. 4859; Sen. bill No. 4135.
[131] Cong. Globe, 42nd Cong., 3rd sess., pp. 11, 15, 853, H. Rept. No. 77.
[132] Ibid., pp. 393, 952, 1549, 2132, H. R. Rept. No. 77.

appointed a committee to determine if any of its members were inculpated.[133]

The resulting testimony brought to light the complicity in the speculation of more outstanding men in public life than any other exposé before or since. Vice-President Colfax, Speaker Blaine, John A. Logan, Roscoe Conkling, Henry Wilson, Henry L. Dawes, John A. Bingham, George S. Boutwell, James A. Bayard, William D. Kelley, James F. Wilson, William B. Allison, James Brooks, James W. Patterson, B. M. Boyer, and Glenni W. Scofield were all affected.

The Poland committee, investigating the conduct of members of the House, found Oakes Ames "guilty of selling to members of Congress shares of stock in the Credit Mobilier of America for prices much below the true value of such stock, with intent thereby to influence the votes and decisions of such members in matters to be brought before Congress for action." [134] Consequently the committee recommended Ames' expulsion from his seat. Likewise James Brooks was expelled for procuring stock for his son-in-law, intended for and applied to his own use and for his own benefit. As a government director he had been doubly culpable for his misconduct. In the Senate the expulsion of Senator Patterson was recommended for contumacy in withholding facts from the committee.

Suspicion of criminal complicity has never been removed from the shoulders of other suspects.[135] Judging the results of the inquiry from a mere political standpoint, it meant a serious set-back to the political careers of James G. Blaine and Schuyler Colfax. By pricking the speculative bubble as early as it did the investigation undoubtedly forestalled a period of much worse deflation than that which actually resulted.

---

[133] Ibid., pp. 1065, 1605, S. Rept. No. 519.
[134] See Oberholtzer, A History of the United States since the Civil War, II, 602.
[135] Ibid., pp. 602-614.

CHAPTER VI

LAW AND PROCEDURE [1]

Uncertainty of the Law of This Subject.—A former Senator from Pennsylvania, George Wharton Pepper, has suggested the confusion which exists concerning the legal phases of Congress' investigative power when, in referring to a book written by Professor Lindsay Rogers he said, " Whatever one's opinion respecting their [congressional investigations] actual utility, it is regrettable that the author does not discuss more satisfactorily the legal questions which they involve. It is not unimportant to determine whether they are or are not legitimate features of our constitutional system." [2] What will be said in this chapter, it is frankly admitted, is by no means the complete explanation which is so much to be desired. If certain phases of the problem can be brought to focus it may aid the ultimate clarification of this much disputed phase of constitutional law.

Investigative Power Warranted Under Implied Powers of the Constitution.—Before examining the limits of the investigative power it is essential to show that such a power exists and that it is a legitimate feature of our constitutional system. It has been pointed out already that the power of Congress to make investigations is nowhere provided for by spe-

---

[1] This chapter has been called " Law and Procedure," rather than the law of congressional investigations. There are two conflicting elements to be considered. First, the limits of Congress' power to investigate, and second, the personal rights and immunities guaranteed to the individual by the Bill of Rights. Here we have two conflicting sets of rights. In the first part of the chapter we shall be concerned with the limits of the power of Congress to investigate, and in the remainder with the rights and immunities of the individual. The importance of procedure is recognized in a consideration of the constitutional guaranties of the individual. We shall find that, since the law is uncertain, because of lack of definite determinations by the courts of the point at which the investigative power ends and the immunites of the individual begin, the customary law is determined in several respects by the procedural prerogatives of congressional committees of investigation.
[2] Harvard Law Review, XL, No. 5 (March 1927), Book Review.

cific provision of the Constitution. That fact, says the strict constructionist, is ample ground for condemning it. In this government of limited powers the Fathers assiduously made provision for all the specific powers which were needed by the National Government to carry out the functions delegated to it by the states. This, they say, is particularly true of the powers of Congress.

This view, although still sometimes expressed, merits little further consideration in light of an impregnable body of law and precedent supporting the opposite contention. The scope of the implied power generally, and of Congress in particular, was most ably stated in the early case of McCulloch *vs.* Maryland, in which the great Chief Justice said:

> It may with great reason be contended, that a government, entrusted with such ample powers (as is the United States) on the due execution of which the happiness and prosperity of the nation so vitally depends, must·be entrusted with ample means for their execution. The power being given, it is the interest of the Nation to facilitate its execution. It can never be to their interest and cannot be presumed to have been their intention, to stay and embarrass its execution by withholding the most appropriate means.[3]

Marshall then goes on to show that the government must be allowed to determine what constitutes appropriate means.

> The government which has the right to do an act, and has imposed on it the duty of performing that act must, according to the dictates of reason, be allowed to select the means. . . . We think the sound construction of the Constitution must allow to the national legislature that discretion, with respect to the means by which the powers it confers are to be carried into execution, which will enable that body to perform the high duties assigned to it, in the manner most beneficial to the people. Let the end be legitimate, let it be within the scope of the Constitution, and all means are appropriate, which are plainly adapted to that end, which are not prohibited, but consistent with the letter and spirit of the Constitution, are constitutional.

The same general principle was early stated in Cohens *vs.* Virginia,[4] with certain pertinently worded deductions which it is timely to note. Marshall stated:

---

[3] 2 Cr. 358; 2 L. ed., 304; W. W. Willoughby, Constitutional Law of the United States, 51, 52.
[4] 6 Wheaton, 264; 5 L. ed. 257.

It is to be observed that it is not indispensable to the existence of every power claimed for the Federal government that it can be found specified in the words of the Constitution, or clearly and directly traceable to some one of the specified powers. Its existence may be deduced fairly from more than one of the substantive powers expressly defined, or from them all combined. It is allowable to group together any number of them and to infer from them all that the power claimed has been conferred.

Then, of prime importance to be noted in view of what has been pointed out above concerning the several functions of congressional investigations, Marshall continues later on, " And it is of importance to observe that Congress has often exercised, without question, powers that are not expressly given nor ancillary to any single enumerated power."

In commenting upon the clause of the Constitution which gives Congress power " to make all laws, which shall be necessary and proper for carrying into execution the foregoing powers," Story ultimately comes to the conclusion that, " Upon the whole, the result of the most careful examination of this clause is, that, if it does not enlarge, it cannot be construed to restrain the powers of Congress, or to impair the right of the legislature to exercise its best judgment, in the selection of measures to carry into execution the constitutional powers of the national government." [5]

Story then has this very challenging thing to say: " If the legislature possesses a right of choice as to the means, who can limit that choice? Who is appointed an umpire, or arbiter in cases, where a discretion is confided to a government?" [6] Story's query suggests concisely one of the principal questions arising from a legal consideration of congressional investigating activity.

There is no doubt that the general doctrine of implied powers is permanently established, or that it has very broad applications. However, in order to prove the justifiability of the implied power to make investigations, it is of course necessary to point to express powers of the Constitution to prove

---

[5] Joseph Story, Commentaries on the Constitution of the United States, III, 123.
[6] Ibid., p. 118.

the validity of each of the three phases of investigative activity.

It was shown above that the implied power to investigate in pursuance of the membership function is based upon the right of each house to judge the qualifications of its members, to discipline them for misconduct, and to protect itself from indignities and interference.

The power of investigation relative to law-making follows from the provision in the Constitution granting Congress all legislative power, and also from the stipulation that Congress shall have power to make all laws which shall be necessary and proper for carrying into execution the powers expressly granted to Congress, the government of the United States, or any of its departments or officers. In practice, of course, it is usually unnecessary to appeal to these general powers, and the validity of the particular investigation can be shown by reference to some specific power, as, for example, the commerce clause.

The power to investigate relative to the executive departments may properly be called, in the writer's opinion, a resulting power. The investigative power is to be assumed from several express constitutional provisions. In the first place, the "necessary and proper" clause, because of the broad interpretation it has received, probably furnishes a valid basis for congressional resolutions of inquiry concerning the actions of executive officials. The power of the House of Representatives to impeach civil officers is the most undebatable express power from which to deduce the implied investigative power.

In addition, the House originates appropriation bills, and the Senate concurs in their passage. It is true that from this power additional powers cannot be adduced. Nevertheless it has been repeatedly argued in committee or on the floor of Congress, usually successfully, that this power furnishes an express constitutional basis for investigations of financial matters. In the recently decided Daugherty case the court refers to the power of appropriation but considers it only as one phase of the general legislative power. This is unquestionably the correct view. The power to appropriate, *per se,* is not a valid basis for an investigation. It is, however, a constituent of the resulting power of investigation.

Likewise, it has been repeatedly argued that since Congress has the power to establish additional departments, and has in fact done so, there is an implied power derived from this implied power to investigate any phase of their activity which seems desirable. This argument, like the one concerning the appropriating power, is valid only when one is speaking of a resulting power of investigation.

Anderson vs. Dunn.—The first case to be considered is that of Anderson vs. Dunn, decided in 1821.[7] This case is not demonstrative of any of the three investigative functions of Congress. It must be considered because this decision was the case of first impression relative to the power of Congress to punish non-members for contempts. It need hardly be suggested that stripped of the power to punish for contempt, Congress' assertion of a power to investigate would be practically void of any real significance. Anderson *vs.* Dunn is so important a landmark that for sixty years thereafter the breadth of the decision was not limited or altered. Its decisiveness undoubtedly warded off an appeal to the courts of several contumacious witness cases, thereby making possible *ad interim* some of the rigorous inquiries we have noted in the chapters above.

The facts in the case of Anderson *vs.* Dunn do not appear in the decision of the court. The constitutional question raised there was the broad one of whether or not the House of Representatives has valid power, under any circumstances, to punish non-members for contempts.

However, it is important to bear in mind that Anderson's contempt did not involve a refusal to give testimony before a committee of investigation.[8] His case was heard before the

---

[7] 6 Wheaton, 204; 5 L. ed. 242.
[8] Cong. Deb., 15th Cong., 1st sess., p. 117; see also "Digest of Decisions and Precedents," Sen. Misc. Docs., 53rd Cong., 2nd sess., ser. No. 3178, p. 35.

bar of the House. The offense which was alleged to constitute a contempt was an offer of a $500 bribe to the chairman of the claims committee.

In the hearing before the House John Anderson was adjudged guilty of contempt and was severely reprimanded by the Speaker. For about ten days preceding this Anderson had been lodged in the common jail, according to the Speaker's orders to one Thomas Dunn, the Sergeant-at-arms.

The case was tried in the Circuit Court for the District of Columbia, and took the form of an action for assault and battery and false imprisonment against said Dunn. Judgment was given for the defendant, whereupon Anderson appealed to the Supreme Court on a writ of error. The opinion was rendered by Mr. Justice Johnson at the February term in 1821.[9] The question, said the court, narrows down to " whether the House of Representatives can take cognizance of contempts committed against themselves, under any circumstances." [10] The court admitted without question that no general power can be found specified in the Constitution, but, " There is not in the whole of that admirable instrument a grant of powers which does not draw after it others, not expressed, but vital to their exercise; not substantive and independent, indeed, but auxiliary and subordinate." [11]

The power to punish for contempt rests upon necessity. For what is the alternative? " The argument obviously leads to the total annihilation of the power of the House of Representatives to guard itself from contempts, and leaves it exposed to every indignity and interruption that rudeness, caprice, or even conspiracy, may meditate against it." [12]

Having determined the above general principles, the arguments of the plaintiff-in-error concerning invalid warrants and personal guaranties were termed minor points. Concerning the warrant, " we are not to presume that the House

[9] 6 Wheaton, 204; 5 L. ed. 242.
[10] Ibid., p. 225.
[11] Ibid., p. 226.
[12] Ibid., p. 228.

of Representatives would have issued it without duly establishing the fact charged on the individual." [13] The bounds of power are the United States, for " such are the limits of the legislating powers " of Congress.

" Public security against the abuse of such discretion must rest on responsibility, and stated appeals to public approbation. Where all power is derived from the people, and public functionaries, at short intervals, deposit it at the feet of the people, to be resumed again only at their will, individual fears may be alarmed by the monsters of imagination, but individual liberty can be in little danger." [14] Moreover, there is an adequate safeguard to the possible abuse of the power of Congress to imprison, because " imprisonment must terminate with that adjournment."

This decision had the effect of recognizing a distinct power of the Houses of Congress to punish contempts. Not until much later, however, was contumacy expressly recognized as a contempt. The court held that both houses of Congress have power to punish contempts which threaten the self-survival of Congress. Each house having jurisdiction of a contempt must determine the fact of such contempt. Whether or not the court would hold this determination irreviewable was not decided definitely until the case of Kilbourn vs. Thompson. A deduction to be drawn from the case of Anderson vs. Dunn is that Congress has a general power to punish for contempt persons disobeying its orders.[15] This inherent power of punishment cannot be used to imprison an offender longer than the adjournment of the particular Congress.

Marshall vs. Gordon.—In this case one finds an attempt by the House to include the writing and publication of a defamatory letter under the privilege of guarding itself from offenses inherently obstructive. The facts were as follows:

H. Snowden Marshall, United States District Attorney for

---

[13] Ibid., p. 234.
[14] Ibid., p. 226.
[15] W. W. Willoughby, Constitutional Law of the United States, II, 1272.

the southern district of New York, was investigated in January, 1916, growing out of impeachment charges brought against him in the House of Representatives.[16] Soon after the committee arrived in New York, Marshall published defamatory charges against the committee. In a letter sent to a New York paper, he alleged that the procedure of the investigation was irregular and extraordinary and that it was simply an attempt to intimidate him from prosecuting the mover of the resolution under the Sherman Act.[17] When he refused to retract these imputations before a committee of reference, Marshall was declared guilty by the House of slander and of contempt of the dignity of the House and of its committee. When Marshall was taken into custody he applied for discharge on habeas corpus. The cause was heard in the District Court of the United States for the Southern District of New York. The correctness of the judgment, refusing the same, was appealed to the United States Supreme Court.[18] Mr. Chief Justice White delivered the opinion.[19] Said the Court:

> Whether the House had power under the Constitution to deal with the conduct of the district attorney in writing the letter as a contempt of its authority, and to inflict punishment upon the writer for such a contempt as a matter of legislative power, that is, without subjecting him to the statutory modes of trial provided for criminal offences, protected by the limitations and safeguards which the Constitution imposes as to such subject is the question which is before us.[20]

After considering the leading preceding cases the conclusion was drawn that such unlimited power—that is, power to deal directly with contempt without criminal prosecution—may be implied from the constitutional grant of power to legislate in so far, and only in so far, as it is necessary to the self-preservation or self-defense of the body.

What, then, is necessary to self-defense? Is the case at

---

[16] Cong. Rec., 64th Cong., 1st sess., pp. 6135-6141 (Jan. 12, 1916).
[17] Ibid., p. 6136.
[18] 235 Fed. 422.
[19] 243 U. S. 521; 61 L. ed. 881.
[20] Ibid., pp. 532-533.

bar such a one? What test, or principles, shall be adopted in determining sufficiency or insufficiency? Self-preservation, the court concludes, is "the right to prevent acts which, in and of themselves, inherently obstruct or prevent the discharge of legislative duty, or the refusal to do something which there is an inherent legislative power to compel, in order that legislative functions may be performed." [21]

Considering the specific facts before it, the court was forced to the conclusion that ill-tempered words might cause irritation and indignation, but that intrinsically they were not of a character to interfere with the legislative process.[22] Therefore the power to punish in this case could not be upheld, even admitting that the House was considering, and its committee contemplating, impeachment proceedings.

Respecting the decision in this case,[23] Professor Burdick says: "It would seem, then, from this opinion, although it

---

[21] The instances of punishment by the Houses of Congress for contempt, which are approved by the court, are instances of "either physical obstruction of the legislative body in the discharge of its duties, or physical assault upon its members for action taken or words spoken in the body, or obstruction of its officers in the performance of their official duties, or the prevention of members from attending so that their duties might be performed, or finally with contumacy in refusing to obey orders to produce documents or give testimony which there was a right to compel" (ibid., 542, 543).

[22] Ibid., p. 547. "The contempt relied upon was not intrinsic to the right of the House to preserve the means of discharging its legislative duties, but was extrinsic to the discharge of such duties."

[23] Two points are brought out by way of obiter dicta which merit some attention. Chief Justice White says: "We think from the very nature of that power it is clear that it does not embrace punishment for contempt as punishment, since it rests only upon the right of self-preservation; that is, the right to prevent acts which, in and of themselves, inherently obstruct or prevent the discharge of legislative duty . . ." (ibid., p. 542).

"Imprisonment only, and for a term not exceeding the session of the body in which the contempt occurred, is the limit of the authority to deal directly by way of contempt without criminal prosecution, implied from the constitutional grant of legislative power to Congress in so far as such authority is necessary to preserve and to carry out the legislative power granted" (ibid., Syllabus, at 4).

"Congressional authority to deal directly by way of contempt without criminal prosecution with acts which interfere with the preservation of its legislative authority does not cease to exist merely because the act complained of may have been committed before the authority is exerted" (ibid, Syllabus, at 5).

is nowhere stated in so many words, that refusal to testify before a congressional committee, which is investigating for the purpose of framing legislation, may be punished as a contempt.[24]

Legality of Investigations Relative to the Membership Function: In Re Chapman.—The Chapman case arose as the result of a Senate investigation conducted respecting the alleged misconduct of certain Senators. In May, 1894, the Wilson-Gorman Tariff Bill was pending the vote of the Senate. It had already passed the House. A very large number of amendments thereto had been appended, but not passed, by the Senate. Among them, certain amendments providing for duties on sugar different from the provisions of the bill as it had been sent to the Senate would appreciably enhance the market value of the stock of the American Sugar Refining Company.[25]

On May 16, 1894, Senator Henry Cabot Lodge introduced a resolution of inquiry which, amended and passed the following day, provided for a committee of five, with power to send for persons and papers, to determine the truth of charges made in the press that certain Senators had been bribed by the sugar interests.[26]

---

[24] Burdick, Law of the American Constitution, 172, 173.

[25] Cong. Rec., 53rd Cong., 2nd sess., pp. 4848-4851; Smith Decisions and Precedents, pp. 583-585.

[26] The amended resolution read as follows: " Whereas it has been stated in the Sun, a newspaper published in New York, that bribes have been offered to certain Senators to vote against the pending tariff bill; and

Whereas it has also been stated in a signed article in the Press, a newspaper published in Philadelphia, that the sugar schedule has been made up as it now stands in the proposed amendment in consideration of large sums of money paid for campaign purposes of the Democratic party, therefore,

Resolved, that a committee of five Senators be appointed to investigate these charges and to inquire further whether any contributions have been made by the Sugar Trust or any persons connected therewith, to any campaign or election purposes or to secure or defeat legislation, and whether any Senator has been or is speculating in

The committee so constituted made several reports. Relative to specific charges which had developed about two Senators, they reported on May 25, 1894: " Your committee find nothing from their investigation to impeach, in the least degree, the honor or characters of Senators Hunton and Kyle." It did appear that during the passage of the tariff most of the principal officers af the American Sugar Company and certain Boston refiners had been active in Washington, but no definite bribery could be established.[27]

Certain it is that the proceedings of the committee were seriously embarrassed by witnesses refusing to testify. No less than seven principal witnesses were adjudged guilty of contempt, and were duly prosecuted in the Supreme Court of the District of Columbia.[28] The case of Elverton R. Chapman finally reached the Supreme Court of the United States on a petition for a writ of habeas corpus, filed on leave.[29]

It appears that Chapman was a stockbroker operating in New York City, and that he was known to have considerable dealings in stocks of the American Sugar Company. His prosecution for contumacy arose upon his persistent refusal to state to the investigating committee whether his firm had or had not bought and sold sugar stocks within a stipulated period of time for or in the interest, direct or indirect, of any United States Senator.[30] In the opinion of the commit-

---

what are known as sugar stocks during the consideration of the tariff bill now before the Senate, and with power to send for persons and papers and to administer oaths.

Resolved further, that said committee be authorized to investigate and report upon any charge or charges which may be filed before it alleging that the action of any Senator has been corruptly or improperly influenced in the consideration of said bill, or that any attempt has been made to so influence legislation " (see Cong. Record, or Smith's Precedents, ibid).

[27] 53rd Cong., 2nd sess., Sen. Rept. No. 606.

[28] Smith, Decisions and Precedents, 587, 805-811.

[29] See also United States vs. Chapman and J. W. Macartney, Supreme Court of the District of Columbia (Smith, op. cit., 797) ; Opinion of Associate Justice Cole, ibid., pp. 805-811; next decided in the court of appeals, District of Columbia, ibid., pp. 822-828; the lower court decisions are reported in 5 App. D. C. 122; 156 U. S. 211 (39: 401) ; 24 Wash. L. Rep. 251, 297, 164 U. S. 436.

[30] The full text may be found in Smith, op. cit., 802-803.

tee and of the Senate such information was germane to the resolution, and therefore Chapman was indictable under Section 102 of the Revised Statutes.

Statutes Respecting Investigations and Punishment of Contempts.—Congress had theretofore enacted legislation more effectually to "enforce the attendance of witnesses on the summons of either House of Congress, and to compel them to discover testimony." On May 3, 1798, Congress provided that oaths or affirmations might be administered to witnesses by the President of the Senate, the Speaker of the House of Representatives, the chairman of the committee of the whole, or the chairman of a select committee, "in any case under their examination." [31]   On February 8, 1817, it enlarged that provision to include the chairman of standing committees.[32]

We have already mentioned the original act of January 24, 1857, stating the circumstances of its passage and its general provisions. This Act provided for certifying contempt cases to the courts, and provided for certain punishments in addition "to the pains and punishments now existing." [33] Again on January 24, 1862, Congress modified the immunity

---

[31] Chapter 36, 1 Stat. at L., Comp. Stat., par. 155; 2 Fed. Stat. Annotated, 2nd ed. p. 532.

[32] Chapter 10, 3 Stat. at L. 345; Comp. Stat. Par. 155; 2 Fed. Stat. Anno. 2nd ed. p. 532.

[33] The act provided, first, that any person summoned as a witness to give testimony or produce papers in any manner under inquiry before either House, who should wilfully make default, or, if appearing, should refuse to answer any questions pertinent to the inquiry, should, in addition to the pains and penalties then existing, be deemed guilty of a misdemeanor and be subject to indictment and punishment of "a fine not exceeding one thousand dollars and not less than one hundred dollars, and suffer imprisonment in the common jail not less than one month nor more than twelve months." Secondly, that no person should be excused from giving evidence in such an inquiry on the ground that it might tend to incriminate or disgrace him, nor be held to answer criminally or be subject to any penalty or forfeiture, for any fact or act as to which he was required to testify, excepting that he might be subjected to prosecution for perjury committed while so testifying (Now Sec. 101-103, Rev. Stat.) Of this act the Supreme Court said that "it was necessary and proper for carrying into execution the powers vested in Congress and in each house thereof." *In Re* Chapman, op. cit., p. 671.

provision in particulars not material here.[34] By Act of June 22, 1874, these enactments were embodied in Secs. 101-104, and Par. 859, Revised Statutes.

The fundamental question before the court was, whether under the resolution authorizing the investigation it could be claimed, as Chapman was contending, that the subject was an improper one for investigation, and that therefore the Senate had exceeded its jurisdiction in attempting to obtain involuntary answers. Considered generally, the court held the view that investigations were prima facie proper in the following cases, appealing to specified or implied provisions in the Constitution for its judgment. " Under the Constitution," the reasoning goes, " the Senate of the United States has the power to try impeachments; to judge of the elections, returns and qualifications of its own members; to determine the rules of its proceedings, punish its own members for disorderly behavior, and, with the concurrence of two-thirds, expel a member; and it necessarily possesses the inherent power of self-protection." [35]

Scrutiny of the provisions of the preamble and resolution convinced the court that this investigation properly fell within the above category, inasmuch as the integrity of the Senate's members had been questioned in such a way as to destroy public confidence, and in such respects indeed as might subject members to censure and expulsion. Said the court, " We cannot regard these questions as amounting to an unreasonable search into the private affairs of the witness simply because he may have been in some degree connected with the alleged transactions, and as investigations of this sort are within the power of either of the two Houses they cannot be defeated on purely sentimental grounds." [36]

It cannot be claimed that the Senate had no power to make the inquiry because the preamble and resolutions did not specify in as many words that the proceedings were taken for

---

[34] Chap. 11, 12 Stat. at L. 333.
[35] 166 U. S. 667; 41 L. ed. 1161; 17 Sup. Ct. Rep. 685.
[36] Ibid., p. 669.

9

the purpose of censure or expulsion. The resolution adequately indicated that the transactions were considered reprehensible and deserving of condemnation and punishment. If the object be proper, the remedy may remain unexpressed.

The remaining objections were easily disposed of. " We grant that Congress could not divest itself . . . of the essenital and inherent power to punish for contempt, in cases to which the power of either house properly extended; but, because Congress, by the Act of 1857, sought to aid each of the Houses in the discharge of its constitutional functions, it does not follow that any delegation of the power in each to punish for contempt was involved; and the statute is not open to objection on that account." [37]

What then of double jeopardy? " It is quite clear, " comes the answer, " that the contumacious witness is not subjected to jeopardy twice for the same offense, since the same act may be an offense against one jurisdiction and also an offense against another. An indictable statutory offense may be punished as such, while the offender may be punished as for a contempt, the two being diverso intuitu and capable of standing together." [38]

Summarizing the court's decision, it appears that the Senate had a right to conduct the investigation in question under its power to expel members for misconduct. Refusal to testify therefore constituted a contempt, which the Senate itself might have punished. Congress might, in addition, make such a refusal to testify a misdemeanor, as it had done in fact by the Act of 1857.[39]

Houses of Congress Have Conclusive Power to Judge Qualifications of Membership.—Whether each chamber has an unlimited right to investigate whatever qualification of a member it may choose, has never been judicially questioned. Indeed the power to judge the qualifications of members,

---

[37] Ibid., p. 670.
[38] For authorities cited by the court in substantiation of this view, ibid., p. 672.
[39] Cf. Burdick, Law of the American Constitution, 172.

although judicial in nature, is vested conclusively in Congress. As Professor W. W. Willoughby points out, " It thus happens that, though neither House may formally impose qualifications additional to those mentioned in the Constitution, or waive those that are mentioned, each may in practice do either of these things. For example, in 1900 the House excluded Brigham H. Roberts of Utah because of various charges brought against him, none of which, however, alleged a constitutional disqualification." [40]

It still remains judicially undecided whether a congressional investigating committee may legally investigate a state primary election for Congress, as did the Reed committee in the Smith and Vare cases. The decision in the Newberry case [41] is not conclusive on this point. As Mr. Pollock concludes, " It seems clear that a portion of the Corrupt Practices Act has been invalidated, but we are not sure that a law passed after the Seventeenth Amendment covering primaries as well as elections would be held void; nor are we certain that the law as applied to Representatives is affected by the decision." [42]

Legality of Investigations Relative to the Law-Making Function.—By the decision of McGrain *vs.* Daugherty, it was conceded that investigating committees of Congress may make inquiry to obtain information for immediate or future legislation. In the earlier case of Kilbourn *vs.* Thompson it was held that the House did not have jurisdiction to make the investigation in question. We shall review both cases. Kilbourn *vs.* Thompson, the next important case chronologically after Anderson *vs.* Dunn, was decided in 1881. The court very much narrowed the limits of the contempt power, holding that a refusal to testify was punishable only in cases where the Houses of Congress were acting in their judicial

---

[40] W. W. Willoughby, Constitutional Law of the United States, I, 525-527. It cannot be questioned that the eligibility of Messrs. Vare and Smith was questioned upon grounds of alleged violation of congressional statutes respecting expenditures, rather than upon grounds mentioned in the Constitution.

[41] 256 U. S. 232.

[42] J. K. Pollock, Party Campaign Funds, 205.

capacities—that is, in reference to election disputes or in impeachment trials. Congress was obviously seeking information, in this case, but it did not appear sufficiently clear that legislation was anticipated. The facts of the investigation were as follows:

On January 24, 1876, the House adopted a preamble and resolution,[43] submitted by Mr. John Glover, of Missouri. Soon after the committee started upon its business one Hallet Kilbourn was summoned before it to testify. Kilbourn was a member of a partnership in the District of Columbia, the real estate firm of Kilbourn & Latta. Jay Cooke & Co., as stated in the resolution, was known to have large real estate interests in the city of Washington. In fact, Kilbourn frankly admitted that Jay Cooke & Co. had put $25,000 into his business.[44] Certain other information, however, Kilbourn refused to divulge.

On March 14, Mr. Glover reported to the House that inasmuch as Hallet Kilbourn had refused to bring certain papers and answer a question as to the whereabouts of the five prin-

---

[43] "Whereas the government of the United States is a creditor of the firm of Jay Cooke & Co., now in bankruptcy by a decree of the district court of the United States in and for the eastern district of Pennsylvania, resulting from the improvident deposits made by the Secretary of the Navy of the United States, with the London branch of said house of Jay Cooke & Co. of the public moneys; and whereas the matter known as the 'real estate pool' was only partially inquired into by the late joint select committee to inquire into the affairs of the District of Columbia, in which the Jay Cooke & Co. had a large and valuable interest; and whereas Edwin M. Lewis, trustee of the estate and effects of the firm of Jay Cooke & Co. has recently made a settlement of the effects of the estate of Jay Cooke & Co. with the associates of the firm of Jay Cooke & Co. to the disadvantage and loss, it is alleged, of the numerous creditors of said estate, including the government of the United States; and whereas the courts are now powerless, by reason of such settlement, to afford adequate redress of said creditors;

Resolved, that a special committee of five members of this House, to be selected by the Speaker, be appointed to inquire into the nature and history of said "real estate pool" and the character of said settlement, with the amount of property involved, in which Jay Cooke & Co. were interested, and the amount paid or to be paid in settlement, with power to send for persons and papers and report to the House" (Reported by Smith, op. cit., p. 536).

[44] Smith, op. cit., p. 538.

cipals of Jay Cooke & Co. he had committed a contempt of the House.[45] The same preliminary report shows that Kilbourn had refused to give the information demanded because it was firmly his conviction that the subject matter was such that the investigating committee did not legally have jurisidction. Upon oath Kilbourn stated that the partnership and the dealings with Jay Cooke & Co. related strictly to private business, in which not a single government dollar nor a sole government official was involved.[46]

The answer of the House was to declare Kilbourn guilty of contempt, and to certify the case as suggested.[47] Kilbourn meanwhile was lodged in the common jail of the District. On March 28, Thompson, the Sergeant-at-arms, reported that upon that day a marshal of the Supreme Court of the District had appeared with a warrant for Kilbourn, preferring criminal charges growing out of the contempt. The House refused to authorize the Sergeant to release Kilbourn under this warrant. Almost two weeks later a writ of habeas corpus was served upon Thompson by the Supreme Court of the District, and not until an additional week had passed did the House accept the recommendation of the Judiciary Committee and authorize Thompson to appear with counsel before the District Court for an opinion.[48] In the judgment of Chief Justice Carter, " with the judgment of the House in contempt, its power to punish terminated, and the punishment prescribed by law intervened." [49] Thereafter the case

---

[45] Ibid., pp. 536-538.
[46] Ibid., pp. 537-538.
[47] Ibid., pp. 541-542.
[48] Ibid., pp. 542-546.
[49] Ibid., p. 552. A portion of this opinion is so suggestive of an important question in the later hearing of the case that it bears stating here. Concerning the charge that trial by the House and the courts constituted double jeopardy the Chief Justice said: " But it is urged, although one offense, it meets several punishments in the several forms for distinct purposes; that the relator is punished in the courts in the penalty of transgression, in the House to make him testify. In one place to visit him with the penalty for what he has done or refused to do in the other place to compel him to do. . . . It is so obnoxious to the common law . . . that they will not even permit confession of guilt under duress." Ibid., p. 551, S. C. Dist. Columbia, 1876 No. 11314, criminal docket.

went in error to the Supreme Court of the United States, where it was decided on January 24, 1881, Mr. Justice Miller delivering the opinion.[50]

In setting about answering the query as to whether or not the House possessed the power to punish the plaintiff-in-error, as for a contempt, upon the facts set out in the special pleas, the court was led to the conclusion that, " The right of the House of Representatives to punish citizens for a contempt of its authority or a breach of its privileges, can derive no support from the precedents and practices of the two Houses of the English Parliament, nor from the adjudged cases in which the English courts have upheld these practices." [51]

In fact the court went on to say that: " The case of Anderson vs. Dunn was decided before the case of Stockdale vs. Hansard, and the more recent cases before the Privy Council to which we have referred. It was decided as a case of the first impression in this court, and undoubtedly under pressure of the strong rulings of the English courts, in favor of the privileges of the two Houses of Parliament. Such is not the doctrine, however, of the English courts today." [52]

" Moreover," continues the reasoning, " the case of Anderson vs. Dunn is no precedent for a case where the plea establishes, as we have shown it does in this case by its recital of the facts, that the House has exceeded its authority." The decision in that case, " though the grounds of the decision are not very clearly stated, we take to be this: that there is in some cases a power in each House of Congress to punish for contempt; that this power is analogous to that exercised by courts of justice, and that it being the well established doctrine that when it appears that a prisoner is held under order of a court of general jurisdiction for a contempt of its authority, no other court will discharge the prisoner or make further inquiry into the cause of his commitment. That this is the

---

[50] 103 U. S. 168, 26 L. ed. 377; Rescinded Feb. 28, 1881; Redecided Feb. 28, 1881, as of Jan. 24, 1881.
[51] 103 U. S. 168; 26 L. ed. 377.
[52] Ibid.

general rule, though somewhat modified since that case was decided, as regards the relations of one court to another, must be conceded." [53] The court concluded, however, that "The tendency of modern decisions everywhere is to the doctrine that the jurisdiction of a court or other tribunal to render a judgment affecting individual rights, is always open to inquiry, when the judgment is relied on in any other proceeding."

That being the case, it follows that, "No person can be punished for contumacy as a witness before either House, unless his testimony is required in a matter into which that House has jurisdiction to inquire." Again, "Neither of these bodies possesses the general power of making inquiry into the private affairs of the citizen."

The court's decision rests largely upon the facts stated in the resolution of inquiry. Does it appear, they ask, that Congress intended to legislate? Did the resolution state this? Was any action intended? Or was this merely a fruitless inquiry? Did the resolution mean the investigation could result in no valid legislation on the subject? [54] The court concluded that it did. "The House of Representatives in passing a resolution reciting that the United States is a creditor of Jay Cooke & Co., and appointing a committee to inquire into the nature and history of the real-estate pool, not only exceeded the limit of its own authority, but assumed a power which could only be properly exercised by another

---

[53] Ibid., p. 178.

[54] The court said: "What was this committee charged to do? To inquire into the nature and history of the real estate pool. How indefinite. What was the real estate pool? It is charged with any crime or offense? If so, the courts alone can punish the members of it. Is it charged with a fraud against the government? Here again the courts, and they alone, can afford the remedy. Was it a corporation whose powers Congress could repeal? There is no suggestion of the kind. . . . Can the rights of the pool, or of its members, and the rights of the debtor, be determined by the report of a committee or by an Act of Congress? If they cannot, what authority has the House to enter upon this investigation into the private affairs of individuals who hold no office under this government?" (ibid., p. 176).

branch of the government, because it was in its nature clearly judicial." [55]

The court therefore concluded that the committee had no lawful authority to require Kilbourn to testify, except in so far as he desired to do so voluntarily. Moreover, the resolution of the House and the warrant of the Speaker were declared void for want of jurisdiction in that body. Kilbourn's imprisonment, therefore, was without lawful authority. So much for the decision with reference to the parties. It was reversed.

The conclusion in reference to the limits of the investigative power are stated cogently in these words:

> This court does not concede that the Houses of Congress possess this general power of punishing for contempt. The cases in which they can do this are very limited. The House of Representatives is not the final judge of its own power and privileges in cases in which the rights and liberties of the subject are concerned, but the legality of its action may be examined and determined by this court.[56]

McGrain vs. Daugherty.—Not until the recent case of McGrain vs. Daugherty was there a frank avowal of the legality of investigations in pursuance of legislation.[57] Kilbourn vs. Thompson held merely that in election disputes or in impeachment trials, in which it would be proper for the house in question to call witnesses, witnesses would probably be subject to the same liability for contempts as they would be before a judicial tribunal. In the Daugherty case the court extended the limits of the investigative power to include investigations which would aid law-making, or which were reasonably calculated at least to assist Congress to legislate at some later time. The significance of the decision is therefore very great. It marks a turning point in the annals of congressional investigations.

The outstanding facts of this case are known rather generally. Harry M. Daugherty became Attorney General March

---

[55] Ibid.
[56] Ibid.
[57] 273 U. S. 135, 71 L. ed. 370.

5, 1921, and held that office until he resigned March 28, 1924. Just prior to his resignation a large part of the time of the Senate was spent in listening to charges of misfeasance and nonfeasance made against him in the Senate chamber.[58] It seemed to be generally conceded that conditions in the Department of Justice were unsatisfactory, and an investigation was looked to by many as the most practicable means of getting at the root of the evil and thereby remedying it or eliminating it.

The first action of the Senate resulted in two measures being passed by both houses, calculated to take certain important measures then being considered, out of the jurisdiction and control of the Department of Justice, and placing them in the hands of special counsel to be appointed by the President.[59] In addition a resolution and two amendments were adopted providing for a select committee of five Senators, " to investigate circumstances and facts, and report the same to the Senate, concerning the alleged failure of Harry M. Daugherty, Attorney General of the United States, to prosecute properly violators of the Sherman Anti-Trust Act and the Clayton Act against monopolies and unlawful restraint of trade; the alleged neglect and failure of the said Harry M.

---

[58] The chief references to these charges are found in Cong. Rec., 68th Cong., 1st sess., pp. 1696, 1698, 1701, 1904, 1976, 2769, 2771, 2881, 2980, 2984, 4412, 10827. As an example of the sort of thing charged, this statement of Mr. Blanton is quoted: " The business of Attorney General Daugherty is to prosecute criminals. Besides the payment of large salaries to his regular employees, his regular attorneys in his Department of Justice, we have given Attorney General Daugherty $500,000 extra of the people's money to prosecute war-fraud cases, and this year we have also given him a special fund to prosecute special cases. What has he accomplished? Whom has he put in the penitentiary? What contract has he broken? What money has he recovered to the Treasury from the expenditure of all these public funds? . . . He had this $850,000 special fund to employ the best lawyers in the United States to do it. Why did he not do it? The only conclusion we can reach is that he did not want to prosecute them. . . . But a man cannot escape doing his duty on the ground of friendship " (ibid., p. 1701).

[59] Cong. Rec., 68th Cong., 1st sess., pp. 1520, 1521, 1728; chap. 16, 43 Stat. at L. 5; Cong. Rec., 68th Cong., 1st sess., pp. 1591, 1974; (Feb. 21, 1924) chap. 39, 43 Stat. at L. 15.; (Feb. 27, 1924), chap. 42, 43 Stat. at L. 16.

Daugherty . . . to arrest and prosecute Albert B. Fall, Harry F. Sinclair, E. L. Doheny, C. R. Forbes, and their co-conspirators in defrauding the government, as well as the alleged neglect and failure of the said Attorney General to arrest and prosecute many others for violations of Federal statutes, and his alleged failure to prosecute properly, efficiently, and promptly, and to defend all manner of civil and criminal actions wherein the government of the United States is interested as a party plaintiff or defendant.

"And said committee is further directed to inquire into, investigate and report to the Senate the activities of the said Harry M. Daugherty, . . . and any of his assistants in the Department of Justice which would in any manner tend to impair their efficiency and influence as representatives of the government of the United States." The resolution also authorized the committee to send for books and papers, to subpoena witnesses, to administer oaths, and to sit at such times and places as it might deem advisable.[60]

In pursuance of its duties and the power granted by the resolution just described, the committee caused to be served upon Mally S. Daugherty, a brother of the Attorney General and president of the Midland National Bank of Washington Court House, Ohio, a subpoena commanding him to appear before the committee to give testimony bearing upon the subject under inquiry, and to bring with him " deposit ledgers of the Midland National Bank since November 1, 1920; also note files and transcript of owners of every safety vault; also records of income drafts; also records of any individual accounts showing withdrawals of amounts of $25,000 or over during above period." [61] The witness did not appear.

Once more the committee summoned Mally Daugherty to appear. This time nothing was said about bringing papers and records. Again the witness disregarded the summons,

---

[60] For the full resolution and two amendments adopted shortly thereafter, see Cong. Rec., 68th Cong., 1st sess., pp. 3299, 3409, 3410, 3548, 4126.

[61] 69th Cong., 1st sess., Sen. Rept. No. 475, p. 7215.

not deigning to send an explanation of any kind in either case.

On April 26, 1924, Mr. Brookhart, the chairman of the investigating committee, reported the facts of the case as regarded M. S. Daugherty to the Senate, with a resolution appended declaring said Daugherty in contempt of the Senate.[62] Thereupon the Senate adopted a resolution setting fcrth the contempt, and authorizing the President pro tempore to issue his warrant and take the recusant witness into custody wherever found.[63]

This subpoena, it will be observed, was intended to obtain only the personal testimony of the witness, and like the second subpoena of the committee, it had no purpose of obtaining the production of books and records originally demanded. In pursuance of his instructions, the Sergeant-at-arms had the warrant issued by his assistant, one John J. McGrain. Daugherty was taken into custody in Cincinnati, Ohio, with the purpose of taking him to Washington, as ordered in the subpoena.

Thereupon the witness petitioned the Federal District Court in Cincinnati for a writ of habeas corpus. The writ was granted and the deputy made due return, setting forth the warrant and the cause of detention. After hearing the case the court held the warrant and cause unlawful, inasmuch as the Senate had exceeded its constitutional powers in ordering the attachment under the terms of the investigation.

---

[62] Ibid.

[63] " Whereas the appearance and testimony of the said M. S. Daugherty is material and necessary in order that the committee may properly execute the functions imposed upon it and may obtain information necessary as a basis for such legislative and other action as the Senate may deem necessary and proper; Therefore be it

Resolved, That the President of the Senate pro tempore issue his warrant commanding the Sergeant-at-arms or his deputy to take into custody the body of said M. S. Daugherty before the bar of the Senate, and then and there to answer such questions pertinent to the matter under inquiry as the Senate may order the President of the Senate pro tempore to propound; and to keep the said M. S. Daugherty in custody to await the further order of the Senate."
Cong. Rec., 68th Cong., 1st sess., pp. 7215-7217.

McGrain thereafter prayed and was granted a direct appeal to the Supreme Court of the United States under Par. 238 of the Judicial Code as then existing.[64]   The decision was rendered January 17, 1927, by Mr. Justice Van Devanter.[65]

The two main issues involved in this case were: first, whether as a broad principle, either or both houses of Congress, or committees of the same, have power, inherent power, to compel individuals to appear before it and give testimony needed " to enable it efficiently to exercise a legislative function belonging to it under the Constitution "; in the second place, whether it appears in this particular case that the process was being employed to obtain testimony for that purpose.

One feature which distinguishes this case from the Kilbourn and Chapman cases is that no questions had been asked by the committee.   Therefore the witness in this case was contending that even assuming the questions which the committee desired to propound were " pertinent and otherwise allowable," there was lacking the original power to summon and compel testimony.

The answer to the first question raised above—that is, as to whether the Senate has an implied power to summon witnesses—allowed little room for speculation.   As we have seen, it has been decisively and consistently answered affirmatively in the leading cases.   Albeit the Court in this decision worked out the ground for the exercise of the implied power through arguments, some of which are novel.   In the method adopted in this case there are the seeds, perhaps, of what may become an increasingly more liberal construction by the courts of the necessity for the particular investigation.

It has been pointed out that two main grounds have been relied upon to sustain the adequate expression of the implied power.   Originally, English precedent was deemed to furnish persuasive argument for an American counterpart.   In the

---

[64] These facts are taken from the statement of the case.   The decision in the court below is found in 299 Fed. 620.
[65] 273 U. S. 135; 71 L. ed., 370.

later cases it was held that the legality of the investigative power in the particular case was to be judged by the necessity and propriety of making the inquiry. This is not to overlook the fact that in all the cases it has been recognized, of course, that any implied power must grow out of one or more constitutional provisions. Thus in this case one is reminded by the court that the Constitution provides that Congress shall have " all legislative powers herein granted," with power " to make all laws which shall be necessary and proper " for carrying into execution these powers and " all other powers, vested by the Constitution in the United States or in any department or officer thereof."

It was Mr. Justice Van Devanter's distinctive contribution that in this case he justified the exercise of the power to summon witnesses by placing great emphasis upon legislative practice, upon investigative precedents if you please. This involved reference to English, colonial, and state precedents, while cases of investigation under the Constitution, especially the early exercise of the power, were principally relied upon.[66] This manner of considering the subject cannot be gainsaid, and it undoubtedly introduces a new emphasis which heretofore has not received adequate cognizance. The court summarizes this point of view as follows: " A long-continued practical construction by Congress of powers under the provisions of the Constitution should be taken as fixing the meaning of such provisions." It is plainly stated that both houses of Congress in their separate relations possess not only those powers specifically provided for in the Constitution, but also such auxiliary powers needed for " the efficient exercise of the legislative function." This investigative power is not an unlimited power—that is, it does not give Congress free rein to delve into the private affairs of individuals—but it is justified in so far as such power is necessary to make express powers effective.

The second main question considered by the Court was concerned with determining whether the particular investi-

---

[66] Ibid., pp. 376-379.

gation in question was such a one as allowed above, namely, an inquiry which was necessary to enable Congress to dispatch its legislative function more efficiently. It thereupon became necessary to determine whether the Circuit Court had judged accurately that the investigation of the Attorney General's office was indeed not allowable because the Senate was attempting to exercise the judicial function. In other words, what was the object of the investigation?

To begin with, said the Court, judging by the resolution, it must be admitted that it is not specifically stated that the object is legislation. However, the Court continues, it does appear that the subject of investigation was the administration of the Department of Justice—whether or not its functions were being faithfully executed. Particularly, its purpose was to determine whether the Attorney General and his assistants were prosecuting certain cases, and whether the will of the legislature was being obeyed in these respects. Specific instances of alleged neglect had been pointed out in the resolution. It was plainly not a general or aimless investigation. There were specific charges, suspicions of misfeasance or nonfeasance. It was not a trial, on the other hand, but merely an attempt to get the facts of an unsatisfactory situation.

It matters not, says the Court, that the resolution did not specifically state the legislative purpose. It must be implied unless there is adequate proof to the contrary. Such is only the established canon of judicial construction. It suffices to show that an investigation would palpably aid legislation which could and probably would result. Then follows an important step in the argument.

That legislation would be aided indirectly, at some future time, is beyond dispute when one recognizes the fact that the Department of Justice, its Attorney General, all his assistants, and every detail of the department are subject to regulation by and report to Congress. It appears to the writer that this is a very realistic and salutary ground upon which to base the argument. Furthermore, the court states that

" the department is maintained and its activities are carried on under such appropriations as in the judgment of Congress are needed from year to year."

In judging the validity of the subject-matter of the investigation it appears that the Supreme Court did not rely upon the content of the resolution as much as did the Circuit Court. The lower court's decision in which the investigation was termed unlawful because of an attempted exercise of judicial power is founded largely upon the stipulation in both Senate resolutions contemplating " other action."

The lower court apparently relied too exclusively upon the terms of the resolutions. The resulting deduction was that the Senate in this case was contemplating action other than legislative, as the outcome of the investigation, at least the possibility of doing so.[67] The Supreme Court, on the other hand, went beyond the resolutions to the subject-matter. Such being the case, the expression " other action " immediately became meaningless and superfluous, because legislation is the only action the Senate could possibly take.[68] We have seen, however, that the court has the broad, the inclusive view of legislation. It was said that it is constantly necessary for Congress to regulate the financial system and the personnel of the departments, as part of the legislative process. In other words, by " legislation " the Court means a great deal more than mere law-making. The Court concludes that the subject-matter of this investigation being

---

[67] Some of the reasons which lead to this conclusion are stated as follows: " The extreme personal cast of the original resolutions; the spirit of hostility towards the then Attorney General which they breathe; that it was not avowed that legislative action was had in view until after the action of the Senate had been challenged; and that the avowal was coupled with an avowal that other action was had in view—are calculated to create the impression that the idea of legislative action being in contemplation was an afterthought . . ." (Quoted by the Supreme Court, Ibid., p. 382).

[68] " We think the resolution and proceedings give no warrant for thinking the Senate was attempting or intending to try the Attorney General at its bar or before its committee for any crime or wrongdoing. Nor de we think it a valid objection to the investigation that it might possibly disclose crime or wrongdoing on his part " (ibid., pp. 283-284).

what it is, the presumption should be indulged that the object was a legitimate one. True, an express avowal of the object would have been preferable, but in the light of the particular subject-matter it was not indispensable.

Now the interesting point to note here is that Mr. Justice Van Devanter once more appreciably extends the focus of the evaluating process in reference to the legality of investigations by placing reliance upon debates in the Senate to mirror the true intent of that body.[69] This method, it appears to the writer, is a very legitimate and useful means of determining the extent to which a particular investigation is justified.

One more point in the decision may be noted. It was pointed out on behalf of the witness that this inquisitorial power, if sustained, might be abusively and oppressively exerted. This argument was countered with the reminder that any power might possibly be abused, but that such a possibility is not conclusive ground for denying its original exercise. Particular abuses must be dealt with as they arise. If either house should violate the rights of witnesses, redress may always be had in the courts, as is demonstrated in the decisions in Kilbourn *vs.* Thompson and Marshall *vs.* Gordon. "And it is a necessary deduction from the decisions in Kilbourn *vs.* Thompson and Re Chapman," the Court continues, "that a witness rightfully may refuse to answer

---

[69] A portion of the debate quoted by the court is given below because of its thought-provoking content. In the course of his remarks Senator George said: " Has not the Senate power to appoint a committee to investigate any department of the government, any department supported by the Senate in part by appropriations made by the Congress? If the Senate has the right to investigate the department, is the Senate to hesitate, is the Senate to refuse to do its duty, merely because the public character or the public reputation of someone whom it is investigating may be thereby smirched? . . . It is sufficient for me to know that there are grounds upon which I may justly base my vote for the resolution; and I am willing to leave it to the agent created by the Senate to proceed with the investigation fearlessly upon principle, not for the purpose of trying but for the purpose of ascertaining facts which the Senate is entitled to have within its possession in order that it may properly function as a legislative body " (ibid., p. 383).

where the bounds of the power are exceeded or the questions are not pertinent to the matter under inquiry." [70]

Courts Should Recognize Validity of the Grand Jury Rôle of Congressional Investigations.—There can be no question that the Daugherty decision appreciably extended the legal power of Congress to investigate. In view of the decision, it seems safe to say that hereafter, all things being equal, Congress may investigate the executive departments with a view to future legislation. It is believed that the Court has done more than this and has at last paved the way for a frank recognition of the validity of investigations which plainly contemplate the possibility of action other than law-making; action, that is, which will assist Congress to hold executive and administrative officials to accountability. Of course, it must be readily admitted that the Daugherty investigation ultimately had a punitive or corrective result. Detecting a punitive intent in the resolution of the Senate, the Court resorted to a subterfuge, namely, the possibility of future legislation, in order to be able to uphold the investigation. It goes without saying that the Senate had little or no idea of future legislation as the principal result of the Daugherty investigation. The concern of the Senate was not with future laws, but with the execution of those already passed.

What was Congress attempting? Was this a trial of Secretary Daugherty? Decidedly not. It was an investigation conceived primarily and almost exclusively to determine the truth or falsity of reports that Daugherty had conspired to escape obedience to the laws of Congress, mandates which ordered him to do certain things in a certain way. [71]

The contention may be made that if " other action " were being contemplated, the only valid basis for an investigation

---

[70] Ibid., p. 382.

[71] Daugherty, of course, had resigned about the time the investigation was begun. What is said here assumes an inquiry in which the official still holds office. Moreover, the writer has no idea that McGrain vs. Daugherty is not good law. What is contended for here is a clarification of the purpose and a recognition of the validity of investigations relative to misfeasance of officials.

10

would be impeachment charges, instituted by the House. Under those circumstances, it would mean that the House alone would have the right to make an investigation.[72] The writer does not accept this view.

In cases such as this the customary practice of both houses of Congress has been to investigate with a view to learning the facts of the situation. No self-crimination of parties investigated is involved. It is not necessary for either House to suggest impeachment in its resolutions. The investigation is merely a fact-finding process preceding regulatory or disciplinary action. The writer believes that investigations of this character are justified on the basis of Congress' resulting power. This resulting power grows out of the several express clauses mentioned at the beginning of this chapter.

There is no reason to assume because Congress investigates that it must take affirmative action to redress the abuse. Unless, as in the Daugherty case, the official chooses to resign, it is appropriate that the President should chastise his subordinate, or that the courts should be given civil and criminal jurisdiction of the case. "Other action," which may lead to corrective action by the President or trial by a federal court, is merely fact-finding. Congress does not transgress the province of the President or of the courts. It merely carries out a grand jury investigation. It is this legal right which the court should recognize, in unequivocal terms.

It may be contended that so long as the validity of the investigation was upheld in the Daugherty case, the mode of reasoning employed is largely immaterial. The rejoinder is that it is conceivable that similar cases may, and probably will, arise in which it will be more difficult for the Supreme Court to uphold the investigation on the basis of the reasoning in this case. Therefore an open recognition of the misfeasance-detecting function of the two Houses of Congress is very desirable.

---

[72] The impeachment trial of Secretary of War Belknap is authority for the view that the House could probably impeach civil officers even after their resignations had been accepted (Cf. Burdick, Law of the American Constitution, 88).

Investigations of executive action are well grounded by long continued practice.[73] This satisfies one of the chief requirements of the Court. In fact, as we have seen, the Court admits that Congress must regulate and reform the executive departments.

If, as we shall see, Congress may by law direct its agent, the Comptroller General, to make investigations of the executive departments, with a view of disciplining officers in addition to obtaining information, why should not the committees of Congress be conceded a legal right to make similar investigations?

Investigations of the executive departments have already effected a degree of cohesion between the excutive domain and Congress which is not inherent in the system of separated powers. If the legality of negligence-detecting investigations of the executive becomes recognized it is not too optimistic a prophecy to assert that investigations may become, to a large extent, the buckle which will bind the executive to Congress.

Investigative Powers of Congress: Summary.—Both Houses of Congress have an implied power to make investigations through committees appointed for that purpose. This is a legitimate feature of our constitutional system. The investigative power is constitutionally implied because it grows out of express powers of the Constitution. Further, it is supported by long-continued practice. There have been more than three hundred investigations in pursuance of the membership, law-making, and executive-regulating functions of Congress. In only three leading federal cases has the investigative power of Congressional committees come sharply into question. In two of these cases the validity of the investigation was sustained. In the other an attempt was made to exceed the legal jurisdiction of the investigative power.

---

[73] For example, consider the investigations of the alleged illegal actions of Secretary of Treasury Wolcott, Secretary of Interior Ewing, Secretary of War Eaton, and of President Buchanan, as discussed in chap. v.

In general, English and American courts have both upheld the investigative power because it is necessary for the survival and efficiency of the legislative process.

But Congress does not possess a general or unlimited power of making investigations. Ours is a Constitution of limited powers. It is true that either house may employ any means necessary in its judgment to the execution of its legislative functions. Nevertheless a valid basis must be proved for making an investigation when a contumacious witness contends that Congress does not have jurisdiction, or that his constitutional rights have been infringed.

Congress undoubtedly acts in a judicial capacity at times. Judging the qualification of its members and their behavior, for example, is so regarded. Moreover, Congress has power to punish the contempts of outsiders. But there is no justification for the contention which is sometimes made that investigations are valid only when either house of Congress is acting in a judicial capacity. Moreover, punishment for contumacy, as punishment, is not a legitimate end of the legislative process. It can only be a means to legislative information.

The power to punish non-members for contempts is, of course, independent of the investigative power. Congress may, instead of or in addition to itself punishing for contempt, provide by law that a contumacious witness be indicted and punished in the courts. This transference possesses advantages for both Congress and the individual.

On the one hand it means that Congress is no longer burdened with vexing and time-taking trials. They were rarely successful in forcing unwilling witnesses to testify and they caused obstruction to the legislative machine. Again, it becomes possible to legislate more severe penalties for contempt, thereby increasing the efficiency of the investigating process. The individual, on the other hand, finds in resort to the courts a release from the arbitrary power of the houses of Congress to pry into his affairs at will and to lodge him in prison.[74]

---

[74] " From 1795, when the House had called to its bar and imprisoned a would-be briber, Congress exercised unchecked for eighty years the power to incarcerate citizens without due process of law " (L. G. McConachie, Congressional Committees, 83).

Finally, by bestowing jurisdiction upon the courts it thereby gives them unlimited discretion to determine the fitness and propriety of the particular adjudicated investigation. It is this power of the courts, and the manner in which they have exercised it that we shall consider next.

The primary question asked in testing the validity of an investigation is whether a legislative object has been set forth in the resolution or resolutions creating the committee. Is the object distinctly specified? Tested by the resolution, is this a public investigation or an inquisition into private affairs? It cannot be said too forcibly that if Congressmen were always far-sighted enough to state a legislative purpose in the resolution, under cover of the same the chances of having the investigation frustrated upon any grounds would become practically nil. The writer is convinced that if the resolution in the Kilbourn case had been more skillfully drafted the decision of the court would have upheld the investigation in that case.

But testing of adequacy does not always stop with appraising the resolution. Specifically in the case of McGrain vs. Daugherty, and possibly unconsciously in the other cases, the Court attached chief importance to the validity of the subject-matter of the investigation. Here the question is, can it be assumed that the subject-matter of the inquiry is necessary and proper to the efficient exercise of the legislative function? Could or would legislation result? Or is the information needed to enable Congress to legislate in the future upon broad questions of finance or organization within the governmental departments?

The presumption is now favorable to allowing a legitimate object when the investigation is concerned with a department or activity of government which Congress has originally created, which it must continue to regulate, and whose continuance is dependent upon Congressional appropriation.

A third test of validity, namely the persuasive force of precedents, was first stressed in deciding contempt cases in the Daugherty case. If Congress has investigated practically the same sort of case several times before, is not the presumption in favor of permitting the exercise of the same power in the contested case? Usually it is. It is fair to insist that precedents should continue to be persuasive rather than increasingly obligatory. The reason for this statement allows opportunity of argument. The view expressed appears the correct one to the writer because it does not seem just or expedient to adopt as conclusive the case of an investigation which has never been legally contested, or perhaps not even resisted before the legislative committee. The right of a legislative body cannot be said to be vested legally, solely by the persuasive force of precedent, until the countervailing constitutional and common law rights of the individual have been adjudicated in a test case based upon the precedent in question. It may be said that acquiescence over a long period implies assent. Acquiescence implies assent, legally speaking, only until the exercise of the power in the particular set of circumstances is contested.[75]

A final test, which as we have seen has been used by the Supreme Court to determine the validity of the contested investigation, is recourse to the debates of the house which created the committee of investigation. We need not here go into the question of the advisability of such judicial construction, as a general rule.[76] It need only be suggested that in contempt cases such action seems peculiarly desirable, and that the presumption is in favor of its efficiency as a sound canon of judicial procedure.

---

[75] The principles of construction involved in this consideration are stated by Professor Willoughby as follows: " The presumption of constitutionality which attaches to an act of Congress is increased when the legislative interpretation has been frequently applied during a considerable number of years, or when it dates from a period practically contemporaneous with the adoption of the Constitution, or when, based upon a confidence in its correctness, many and important public and private rights have become fixed.

" The Supreme Court has, however, never held itself absolutely bound by a legislative or executive construction (political questions excepted) however long acquiesced in, or however nearly contemporaneous in its first statement with the adoption of the Constitution." W. W. Willoughby, Constitutional Law of the United States, I, 25, 26.

[76] Ibid., I, 33.

It appears reasonable in construing such action by the court to draw an analogy to the accepted rule of construction whereby when constitutional questions arise great reliance is placed upon the debates of the Constitutional convention or upon debates in Congress shortly following. The purpose is the same. The Court does not take recourse to the debates with pre-conceived suspicions of detecting a purpose other than legislative as the object of the investigation, but simply to throw more light upon a constitutional object set out in the resolution, or to substantiate the validity of the subject-matter where the object is not specifically avowed. In other words, validity is assumed. Reference to debates seeks but to establish the presumption. Yet, inasmuch as a question of jurisdiction is involved no self-imposed limits should be built up by the courts to hamper the full exposition of the real object of the investigation.

Investigative Power of Congressional Committees Not Subject, by Analogy, to Limitations Upon Investigations by Administrative Commissions.—It appears that the Revised and Annotated Constitution, issued by the authority of the Sixty-eighth Congress, does not overstate the case when it concludes that, " The powers of Congress in respect to investigation and legislation are not absolutely identical, but the power of investigation is the wider and extends to matters on which it could not constitutionally legislate directly, if they are reasonably calculated to afford information useful and material in the framing of constitutional legislation."

However, with respect to upholding the investigative power of commissions created by Congress, the courts have been far less liberal.[77] As a result, repeated attempts have been made

---

[77] The limits of the investigative powers of the Interstate Commerce Commission and of the Federal Trade Commission are considered broadly in the important cases of Brimson vs. I. C. C. (154 U. S. 447, 28 L. ed. 1047); Harriman vs. I. C. C. (211 U. S. 407, 53 L. ed. 253); United States vs. Louisville & N. R. Co. (236 U. S. 318, 59 L. ed. 598); and Federal Trade Commission vs. American Tobacco Co. (264 U. S. 298, 68 L. ed. 6). The court has held that these commissions do not have power to make fact-finding investigations as such, but that in order to prove legal justification for the

to argue that the powers of congressional committees, by analogy, are similarly limited.   The contention is ridiculous.

The general limitations laid down in these commission cases do not affect analogously the powers of congressional committees because the legal basis of congressional committees is found in implied powers of the Constitution, whereas the rights of commissions are strictly circumscribed by statute. In the second place, the assumption of validity which attaches to acts of Congress does not attach in like measure to the acts of administrative boards.   Finally, the purpose of Congress is legislation, which entails fact-finding, whereas the primary function of these commissions is enforcement, involving prosecutions at law.

Just as adjudications concerning the investigative powers of federal administrative commissions cannot be taken to minimize the power of Congress to investigate through its committees,[78] the decisions in state courts relative to legislative investigations cannot be considered to increase the pre-

---

investigation it must be shown that a specific breach of a federal law is involved. For instance, in the Harriman case it was stated that "the power to require testimony is limited, as it usually is in English-speaking countries, at least, to the only cases where the sacrifice of privacy is necessary . . . those where the investigations concern a specific breach of the law" (211 U. S. 407).   There can hardly be any question that, as suggested in the dissenting opinion in this case, the Court has narrowed the powers of these commissions in relation to the laws establishing and empowering them, and in the face of the clearly expressed intentions of Congress that they should make fact-finding investigations. This view is brought out forcibly in Mr. Justice Day's dissent (ibid., p. 419).

[78] With respect to some matters there can be no doubt that the courts would hold determination in commission cases of strong persuasive force in deciding the same point in congressional cases. For example, the Court inferred in the Daugherty case that if the committee had persisted in demanding all papers and documents from the Midland National Bank, that the court's decision in this respect would have followed a rule similar to that of Federal Trade Commission vs. American Tobacco Company.   In the case just referred to the Court stated the rule concerning the right of demanding documents as follows: "The right of access by the statute is to documentary evidence,—not to all documents, but to such documents as are evidence. The analogies of the law do not allow the party wanting evidence to call for all documents in order to see if they do not contain it. Some ground must be shown for supposing that the documents called for do contain it" (264 U. S. 306).

sumption in favor of an unlimited Congressional power of investigation. Congress has only such powers as are delegated to it, while the state legislatures have full powers within their jurisdictions.

Personal Guaranties.—Questions of personal guaranties, as we shall discover, are in many cases inextricably bound up with problems of committee procedure. To begin with, it may be stated as a general proposition that the Constitutional guaranties relative to trials do not control the rules of procedure within the congressional chamber. Investigations, it may bear repeating, are not trials. Therefore the rules of a court of law do not apply. This was early decided in the cases of Robert Randall and William Duane, in 1795,[79] and in the famous case of John Smith, a Senator from Ohio, in the same year.[80] Since then the question has been raised repeatedly, but the decisions by the committees, the two houses, and the courts have been uniformly insistent in declaring that the two houses of Congress were not bound to follow the principles nor the precedents of courts of law in conducting investigations.[81]

Fourth Amendment.—Where privacy has been contended for, witnesses have relied principally upon the provisions of the Fourth Amendment. This states that:

The right of the people to be secure in their persons, houses, papers and effects, against unreasonable searches and seizures shall not be violated, and no warrant shall issue but upon probable cause, supported by oath or affirmation, and particularly the place to be searched, and the person or things to be seized.

The question of unreasonable searches and seizures is resolved into a determination of the commitee's jurisdiction in making the investigation, and of whether the witness' testimony and documents are pertinent thereto. If it can be proved that the committee has jurisdiction of the case, the

---

[79] Smith, Precedents, op. cit., pp. 3-18.
[80] Ibid., pp. 19-21.
[81] Hinds' Precedents, III, Sects. 1813-1821.

provisions of the amendment are in most cases no bar to the demands of the commitee.

It has already been noted in the above cases that the personal guaranty in respect to the issuing of subpoenaes duces tecum by investigating committees and of warrants by the Speaker is more liberal than the common law rules on the subject. Although oaths and affirmations affirming a good and sufficient cause need not be set out in the warrant, the courts have held the same legal without exception, because, they say, it must be assumed that the committee having been commissioned with the power of the house and knowing the facts for which the witness is summoned will issue the warrant only upon probable and sufficient provocation.[82]

The arbitrary power of committees to demand the production of papers, once the power has been granted by the house, has been the chief subject of denunciation by witnesses throughout the history of investigations. An instance, not at all unusual, of the breadth of the demands for the papers of the witness, his characteristic reply, and the justification of such action by the committee is cited in the footnote.[83]

---

[82] Cf. especially the Kilbourn and Daugherty cases above.

[83] In pursuance of their duties to conduct an investigation relative to alleged abuses by the Treasury Department in relation to deposit banks, one R. M. Whitney was summoned, January 23, 1837, to testify as one of the suspected agents of the deposit banks (Journal, 24th Cong., 2nd sess., 164; Globe, pp. 69, 73).

In the course of the investigation Whitney was ordered to bring with him, " the books, papers, and memoranda relating to his agency with the deposit banks; that he produce all the correspondence between himself and any person or bank going to show the existence of that agency; that he produce the originals, where in his power, and copies where the originals are not in his possession; that he produce all the contracts which he has made or proposed with and to any bank, or correspondence held with relation to the public deposits; all books, papers, etc. going to show the amount of his compensation, and the character of the business which he is employed to transact " (24th Cong., 1st sess., House Report No. 193, p. 2). In spite of an objection on the part of Mr. Martin that such a demand was not justified according to the showing then before the committee, the resolution was passed without further objection.

On January twenty-fifth, Whitney, who had already refused to answer certain questions, filed a protest with the committee relative to the demands for the production of papers. The demand, he says, " searches into the documents of my business and transactions—

Reference to the demand of the committee in the Daugherty
case for the production of papers and deposit records, a request never carried to fruition, shows that although the demands were broad there is found a careful designation of
the particular papers and records desired. This tendency
toward definiteness is of fairly recent origin, and one to be
heartily commended. It is interesting to note that in 1876,
after examination and discussion, the House decided, and it
is still the rule, that there is nothing " in the law rendering
a communication transmitted by telegraph any more privileged than a communication made orally or in any manner
whatever. [84]

The attitude of investigating committees relative to the
production of papers has been even more insistent in respect
to public officers. This demand to produce evidence against

---

sweeping up even the loose memoranda I may have kept relating to
my agency (no matter to what other things the same memoranda
may relate). . . ." He suggests that the limit of that power as
respects private persons may be summarized as the power to demand,
" such private papers in the hands of individuals as are necessary
to the advancement of justice in the exercise of the judicative power
of Congress, understanding that power to be limited to impeachment.
Then such private papers, and such only, are included as would, if
produced, be competent evidence in a criminal prosecution and in
a prosecution not against the party cited to produce the papers. . . .
The paper required must be described with reasonable certainty, so
as to be distinguished and identified; above all, it must be made
clearly to appear, before its production is required, to be competent
and pertinent evidence to the issue, or, if the issue be not yet formed
(as in the case of a presentment pending before a grand jury or an
impeachment in course of preparation), still competent and pertinent
evidence to the issue to be formed, in case the presentment be found
true, or the impeachment be preferred." Ibid., p. 1 ff.; Hinds, III, 96.
  Whitney's refusal to produce this large and miscellaneous mass
of private papers appeals to one as justifiable. This point of view,
although not conceded by the committee, was approached at least.
They finally stated that the terms of the demand had been made
general because they did not know just what papers Whitney possessed, and that " they thought it due to the witness himself that he
might have the opportunity of producing such papers of a private
character as he might deem necessary for the purpose of explanation
if such explanation should be deemed necessary by him." They concluded with an avowal that in this case the " safety of the public
funds " makes it imperative that the witness should produce all the
papers ordered in the original resolution (Hinds, III, 96).
  [84] Cong. Rec., 44th Cong., 2nd sess., pp. 244, 324-330.

oneself, it has been seen, was vehemently denounced by President Jackson in the broad investigation of the executive departments in 1837. [85] As a result of his attack the committee stated that in their opinion Congress had a vested right to supervise the acts of its agents, carrying with it the privilege of calling upon them for any records indicative of failure to comply with the law.

They deliberately rejected the idea of demanding statements touching motives and acts not shown to be unlawful, if proved, and papers which are private in their character, " and not coming within the denomination of papers on file. " [86] In the matter of deciding what constitutes a private matter, they said, a large degree of discretion must be permitted the public servant. However, if he abuses that discretion the officer must be held responsible for it in some other form of investigation into his official conduct.

In authorizing an investigation of the Bank of the United States in 1832 a distinction was drawn between the public relations of the bank to the government and its dealings with private parties.[87] Despite this precaution, John Quincy Adams, of Massachusetts, the persistent critic of the investigation and the first outstanding challenger of an unlimited power of investigation, showed that the majority of the committee did not follow the distinction, but investigated the personal accounts of individuals, such as several proprietors of well-known newspapers. [88]

Abuses like this are probably inevitable. As the court stated in the Daugherty case, abuses must be corrected as they arise, without summarily condemning the power because they are entailed. The cry of unreasonable search or embarrassing exposure of private affairs possesses shallow content in the face of an investigation which can be proved to demand the production of information needed in a legitimate inquiry.

---

[85] Cf. Hinds, III, 99-101.
[86] Ibid.
[87] Hinds, III, 86.
[88] Ibid.; See also Landis, op. cit., 179-182.

In the past, not even members of the coördinate house have been entirely immune. In the investigation of 1837 the chairman of the House committee caused three Senators to be subpoenaed. [89] One of them, Calhoun, respectfully declined. The two others, however, appeared at the stipulated time and before testifying contented themselves with filing a protest on the records of the committee. The general rule in cases where the testimony of members of the opposite house is wanted is to obtain leave of the particular house for the members concerned to attend.[90]

Self-incriminating Evidence.—By a stipulation of the Fifth Amendment it is provided that no witness in any criminal case shall be made to give testimony or evidence which would incriminate himself. By the Act of 1857 making contempt for refusal to testify a criminal offense (now incorporated in 101-103 Rev. Stat.), Congress has provided that " no person should be excused from giving evidence in such an inquiry on the ground that it might tend to incriminate or disgrace him, nor be held to answer criminally or be subjected to any penalty or forfeiture, for any fact or act as to which he was required to testify, excepting that he might be subjected to prosecution for perjury committed while so testifying. " Through this provision Congress has made inquisition possible, while at the same time the witness is protected from the possible penalties arising from his disclosures.

The policy of investigating committees in recent years has been to refrain from summoning persons whose conduct is being investigated. At times, as in the case of the Sinclair scandal, those principally involved have been heard voluntarily. Probably the chief reason for this caution is that records of investigating committees may be introduced as evidence in consequent civil or criminal proceedings. Care is therefore taken not to vitiate the record.

---

[89] Hinds, III, 130.
[90] Ibid., p. 129. For an exception to this rule see ibid., p. 133. The House has, by resolution, demanded of certain of its members the production of papers (ibid., p. 138).

With reference to giving evidence concerning corporations, the rule stated in Boyd vs. United States [91] would seem to apply, quite irrespective of Congressional statute. The power of Congress to investigate was not involved in the Boyd case. The decision in no way limits the rule stated above, but rather is in general accord. Since a corporation is a creature of the State, and the state has more freedom in investigating its conduct than that of a natural person, the production of the corporation's papers may be compelled, though they may tend to incriminate it. [92] Furthermore, an officer of a corporation may not refuse to produce the books or papers under his charge or in his possession on the ground that they will tend to incriminate him.[93]

Hearings not Necessarily Speedy nor Public.—In the light of what has been said concerning the dissimilitude of congressional investigations and public law trials, it need hardly be suggested that committees of inquiry are under no compulsion to make their hearings either speedy or public. A witness may be called every day the committee convenes.

Likewise with regard to the hearings, the committee has discretion to make them secret and in several cases such committees have even obtained the consent of the chamber to keep their records and reports secret.[94]

Giving Evidence in Own Behalf Dependent upon Committee.—Likewise with regard to the matter of giving evidence in one's own behalf, a great deal depends upon the will of the committee. Experience has proved that the most effective way for a witness to express independent ideas, disapprobation, or to submit evidence, is to obtain the consent of the com-

---

[91] 116 U. S. 616 (1886).

[92] Hale vs. Henkel (1906) 201 U. S. 43. It is interesting to note that it was held in this case that an order for the production of papers may be so sweeping and unreasonable as to be unconstitutional. This question has never been passed upon in cases of investigation.

[93] Wilson vs. United States (1911) 221 U. S. 361; Wheeler vs. United States (1913), 226 U. S. 478; Grant vs. United States (1913), 227 U. S. 74.

[94] Hinds, III, 138.

mittee to present a written statement by himself or counsel. It rests entirely with the committee how much force this will eventually have in moulding the committee's report. As will be pointed out presently, however, this method is far superior to relying upon a chance to express one's untrammeled convictions audibly.

The witness may call other witnesses in his behalf, as a rule, by permission of the committee, but not of inherent right. Here too the investigating committee assumes complete control of the procedure. Prior to 1861 there were constant complaints by House committees that witnesses had appeared who had not been summoned by order of the committee. Largely to alleviate this condition, the select committee to investigate the subject of executive influence over legislation, corruption in elections, etc., ordered that "witnesses shall be summoned pursuant to the order of the committee; and that the Clerk shall enter upon the journal of this committee the name of the witness so ordered to be summoned, at the time such order shall be made."[95] Such is the origin of the present rule in this respect. As for the protection afforded in the Constitution against double jeopardy, the rule in that respect has already been noted above.

Use of Counsel Regulated by Committee.—In the very important matter of permitting the witness to be advised by counsel, the rule has varied appreciably. In the earliest cases noted above, those of Robert Randall, Charles Whitney, and William Duane, the witnesses were allowed to leave the room in the discretion of the committee and ask the advice of counsel awaiting them.[96] However, when James W. Simonton appeared before Mr. Orr's committee which was investigating charges of bribery against members of the House, in 1857, the witness was repeatedly denied permission to consult counsel who attended him.[97] In 1876 the House,

---

[95] Ibid., p. 136.
[96] Smith, op. cit., 1-18.
[97] 34th Cong., 3rd sess., H. R. Rept. No. 243, pp. 175-182.

on the recommendation of the Judiciary committee, passed a resolution whereby only those lawyers or agents could be called upon who in advance should have filed their names and authority with the clerk of the House.[98]

An instance of a comparatively liberal attitude as regards the presence of counsel is found in the case of James E. Anderson, who on June 4, 1878, was a witness before the select committee appointed to investigate the presidential election of 1876. Anderson was accompanied by counsel, who sat behind him and consulted with him during the examination.[99]

Mr. Hinds records what he deemed a manifestation of great " latitude " by a committee, in the matter of permitting recourse to counsel. [100] It seems that in 1878 the House select committee on Alleged Frauds in the Presidential Election of 1876 permitted John Sherman, Secretary of the Treasury, whose conduct was being investigated, to be represented by counsel. Mr. Shellabarger, Sherman's attorney, was not permitted to ask questions, however, and questions which he desired to ask were required to be communicated through some member of the committee.[101]

The writer knows of a more liberal construction than the above which occurred about the same time. In the examination of Hallet Kilbourn, Mr. Black, his attorney, was permitted to take the stand and cross-examine his client. This was done without the interposition of questions by the committee members. Through the examination Mr. Black was able to establish what Kilbourn had been unable to do unassisted because of objections by the committee, namely to point out that there was nothing in the nature or history of the real estate pool, connected with any public affair, but that the partnership of which he was a member was purely a private matter. [102]

---

[98] Cong. Rec., 44th Cong., 1st sess., p. 3230.
[99] 45th Cong., 3rd sess., H. Misc. Doc. No. 31, I, p. 48.
[100] Hinds, III, 128.
[101] 45th Cong., 3rd sess., H. Misc. Doc. No. 31, p. 11.
[102] Smith, op. cit., 537.

Ex Parte Inquisition.—This question of permitting counsel to witnesses and of allowing cross-examination by them
appears to the writer as the crux of investigative procedure.
Despite the fact that investigating committees are not expected
to follow the rules of a law court, it appears nevertheless
inexcusable to gather a mass of accusatory statements from
witnesses, many of whom are prone to be actuated by malice
or given to easy gossip, without later or at the time giving
the party accused or other witnesses opportunity to come face
to face with accusing witnesses, who may be interrogated by
the accused's counsel.

The immediate rejoinder is that an investigation is not a
trial, and that if cross-examination is desired the case can
be brought before a court of competent jurisdiction, permitting an adequate defense. But what, it may be asked, is the
purpose of hearings before investigating committees? Is
their purpose vindictive, ex parte, a consuming passion to
establish evidence of guilt at all costs? Or is it rather to
examine the facts of the particular case, pro and con, enabling
the committee to render a judicious report to an assembly
requiring unbiased facts?

If the purpose is the latter, then witnesses should be
permitted to confront the accuser, and cross-examination
should be frankly permitted. Competent precedent is found
for this view in an early outstanding case already considered,
that of General Wilkinson. The original investigation was
entirely ex parte. Realizing that such procedure outraged
the sensibilities of freemen and the spirit of the Constitution,
a second investigation was launched in which Wilkinson was
allowed ample opportunity to state his case and to face his
accusers.[103] There has been a growing tendency of late
years to permit witnesses greater liberty to consult counsel.

The rule in reference to the use of counsel and the possibility of cross-examination of interested witnesses, as it is
usually interpreted in practice today, is this: It is altogether

---

[103] 11 Ann. Cong., part 2, pp. 1616, 2288; second investigation, ibid.,
3rd sess., pp. 432, 1039 (1810).

11

customary for the committee to permit witnesses to be cross-examined by counsel for any person appearing to be interested. This was true, for example, of the Teapot Dome inquiry, during which Mr. Sinclair's counsel was accorded that privilege.

Far too many early cases might be cited where justice has not been done in these respects. For instance, in the famous investigation cited above, that of alleged corrupt combinations of members in 1857, the committee without warrant proceeded to place three members of the House virtually on trial, culminating their ex parte hearings by submitting resolutions for the expulsion of the accused members. Complaints from the outraged members were profuse.

Charges like the above, of "secret ex parte inquisition," are the most damaging charges concerning investigations which must be faced by the constructive student of their procedure.[104] The inquisitorial attitude which is so prone to pervade the countenance of investigations is undoubtedly conducive to convictions, but it repulses competent and unbiased knowledge. [105] The witness is utterly at the mercy of

---

[104] It is interesting to note in passing that during a Senate debate in 1860 Charles Sumner came forth flatly with the statement that the House possesses the inquisitorial power, but that the Senate on the other hand is precluded from the exercise of such a power. His reasoning is summarized in the following quotation: "We must not forget a fundamental difference between the powers of the House of Representatives and the powers of the Senate. . . . To the House of of Representatives are given inquisitorial powers expressly by the Constitution, while no such powers are given to the Senate. This is expressed in these words, 'The House of Representatives shall have the sole power of impeachment.' Here, again, obviously, is something delegated to the House, and not delegated to the Senate— namely, those inquiries which are in their nature preliminary to an impeachment—which may or may not end in impeachment; and since, by the Constitution, every 'civil officer' of the general government may be impeached, the inquisitorial powers of the House may be directed against every 'civil officer' from the President down to the lowest on the list.
This is an extensive power, but it is confined solely to the House. Strictly speaking, the Senate has no general inquisitorial powers." Cong. Globe, 36th Cong., 1st sess., p. 3007; Quoted by Hinds, III, 77.
[105] During an investigation by a committee, if a question is objected to, the committee decides whether or not it shall be put. The

the austere panel of committeemen.   There is no escape from the customary procedural rules.   The witness has no inherent rights, but must rely upon the committee for privileges.   The witness must tell all, or face the possibility of a jail sentence and a heavy fine.   Subsequently he is not liable to prosecution as a natural person, but he must consider well his replies, or else be prosecuted for perjury.   In view of these facts, it is suggested that the thing most needed in congressional investigations is a constant recognition on the part of committeemen of the enormity of the power exercised, and of the corresponding trust incurred in respect to the rights and sensibilities of the citizen.[106]

---

rule stated applies of course to objections by members of the committee and not to protests by witnesses.   In case of an objection the chairman says, " Shall the question be received? "   Thereupon a vote is taken *viva voce.*   An example of this rule of procedure is found in the records of the committee which was investigating the attack upon Senator Sumner (see Hinds, III, 123).   A further rule on the subject is that a question proposed to be propounded by a member of a committee directly to a witness should not be amended, but should be allowed or rejected in its original form (ibid., p. 122).   Questions are agreed upon in advance and are put by the chairman.

[106] The darkest spot on the investigative escutcheon, it is generally known, was the treatment meted out to Reuben Whitney at the hands of a committee in 1837.   Adams' diary records the scene as follows: " When Reuben Whitney was before a committee of investigation in 1837, Bailie Peyton, of Tennessee, taking offense at one of his answers, threatened him fiercely, and when he rose to claim the committee's protection, Mr. Peyton, with due and appropriate profanity, shouted, ' You shan't say one word while you are in this room; if you do I will put you to death.'   The chairman, Henry A. Wise, added: ' Yes, this insolence is insufferable.'   As both of these gentlemen were armed with deadly weapons, the witness could hardly be blamed for not wanting to testify again " Adams' Diary, XII, 162; Quoted in Alexander, History and Procedure of the House of Representatives, 116.

CHAPTER VII

CRITICISM AND FORECAST

Principal Criticisms of Investigations.—Many and varied
are the invectives hurled against congressional investigations.
Even so shrewd a political observer as Woodrow Wilson was
in many respects satisfied himself with accepting the popular
derogatory idea of them. Says he: " Congress cannot control
the officers of the executive without disgracing them. Its
only whip is investigation, a semi-judicial examination into
corners suspected to be dirty. It must draw the public eye by
openly avowing a suspicion of malfeasance, and must then
magnify and intensify the scandal by setting its committees
to cross-examining scared subordinates and sulky ministers.
After all is over and the murder is out, probably nothing is
done. The offenders, if anyone has offended, often remain in
office, shamed before the world, and ruined in the estimation
of all honest people, but still drawing their salaries and com-
fortably waiting for the short memory of the public mind to
forget them. Why unearth the carcass if you cannot remove
it? "[1]

The public generally disposes of the occasional investigative flurry with the epithet, " another fishing expedition."
The man who is in a position to know the deeper significance of investigating activity sometimes finds himself concluding that after all they are just " a scavenger of the private drains responsible for public malady." What content
of truth is there in these and other similar charges?

One of the most common criticisms of Congressional committees of investigation is that they are used for political purposes.[2] This criticism would not be ill-founded if it were not

---

[1] Woodrow Wilson, Congressional Government, 271, 278.

[2] It is frequently said that investigations merely collect " gossip " which no law court would admit. There is unfortunnately a
great deal of truth in this charge. On the other hand, gossip has
in some important cases served the cause of justice. It is believed

assumed at the same time that party bias is the one and only explanation of investigations. Consider, for example, the prevalent ideas concerning the major investigations of the first session of the Seventieth Congress. The press invariably summed up the situation with the statement that these investigations were aimed solely at "turning up mire for the 1928 political campaign." This statement undoubtedly has a large portion of truth in it. It is unfortunate that it is still generally thought that party motives are an evil which unfortunately must be endured. If there were nothing more to investigations than party biases they would still probably be worth the price which we pay for them.

After all, does it matter so much whether the investigation serves political purposes if the end is beneficial, and the conduct of it is above-board? Is not such a motive inevitable, and of infinite value? Is it not possible that investigations may have practical as well as political services to perform, both of them legitimate? Although it is impossible to state positively the extent to which party spleen controls the inauguration of investigations, research in the records does convince one that there is surprising lack of antagonism in the conduct of inquiries. Is it not worthy of remark that in the conduct of inquiries so prone to be inquisitorial and bitter, the number and vehemence of minority reports is so disproportionate? If one were to compare the reports of the principal investigations with the commonly accepted leading constitutional decisions it would undoubtedly be discovered that the number of minority dissents would compare favorably.

Sometimes investigations are criticized because it becomes necessary to travel to distant parts of the country. True, but are there ample grounds to condemn such a practice for that fact alone? Many times, as in the cases of the Kansas troubles, and the Louisana riots, traveling to the scene is the only way of obtaining the desired information.

---

that loose talk is not necessarily an ineradicable defect of the system, but that it can be prevented by the committee's rules of procedure.

The very size of the country and its manifold interests complicate the difficulties of lawmaking. Such being the case, investigations which involve travel should be tested by their success in divulging information rather than by the number of times the car wheels revolve.

One implication of this charge of wasting time is shared, in large part, by the writer. In time-consuming inquiries, some have found another costly diversion, which, coupled to the necessity of Congress' making minute regulations for the Army and Navy and fifty other executive agencies in Washington, and especially for the administration of the District of Columbia, halts the legislative machine and results in leaving unaccomplished every session much important business.[3]

When the proposal for a Senate committee to investigate the S-4 disaster came up in the Senate in January, 1928, it was frequently said in debate, and undoubtedly with a good deal of basis in fact, that there were not enough Senators left at that time who were not otherwise engaged in some other investigation to make such an investigation possible. It is believed that the Senate will soon learn the limit of human and Senatorial capacity and take steps to alleviate some of the burdens of committees of investigation. The first step in this direction is contemplated in a resolution recently introduced by Senator Walsh of Montana. The resolution which was adopted by the Senate January 24, 1928, obviates the necessity of Senators going outside of Washington to hold hearings. Provision is made to permit specially appointed commissions to take testimony outside the United States also. The resolution gives the Vice-President authority to appoint commissions to hold hearings for any Senate investigations in any part of the country.

A third criticism of the procedure and results of congressional investigations is that they do not include technical experts among their personnel. The result, it is alleged, is that in many cases the committees of Congress are incompetent to deal with the situation at hand. The criticism is

---

[3] Lindsay Rogers, The American Senate, 195-197.

well taken. Its solution is simple and obvious. There is no reason whatever why Congress should not include technical experts in the personnel of its committees when it sees fit. It is believed that the tendency is in that direction, as proved by the S-4 investigation, for instance. The procedure would then be for the expert to reveal the facts, and for the congressional members of the committee to absorb, criticize, and report these findings.

Granted that Congressional investigations have accomplished something, says the critic of them, yet is it not true that the inordinate cost of inquiries, growing constantly greater, is disproportionate to their net accomplishments? It may be pointed out, for instance, that during the first six months of 1926 the official figures of the secretary of the Senate show that the Senate alone spent $121,147.38 for investigations. Furthermore it may be pointed out that of this total expenditure a large proportion was spent by three committees which traveled to the far west.

Traveling and hotel expenses alone for these three investigations, although a relatively small part of the total expense, came to over six thousand dollars for the Colorado River inquiry; to almost four thousand dollars for an investigation of forest reserves; while the committee which traveled west to ascertain the effect of the postal rate increase in various parts of the country spent almost seven thousand dollars for these two items.

Furthermore, runs the indictment, during this same period one lawyer attached to the forest reserve investigation drew $4,900, at the rate of fifty dollars a day. Then, to top the preposterousness of such needless expenditures, the figures record in indisputable fashion the fact that it cost the government more than a thousand dollars to bring W. S. Culberson to this country from Rumania, where he resided as Minister, to testify in the investigations of the tariff commission, of which he was formerly a member. Of this amount three hundred sixty-six dollars was remuneration as a witness at six dollars a day. Witnesses before Senate committees usually draw only three dollars a day.

Similar figures, it may be observed, may be found demonstrating the vast sum needlessly wasted because of the English "question time." The analogy is pertinent. It is generally conceded that the worth of the English question cannot be measured in dollars and cents. Certain it is also that congressional investigations have at times saved to the taxpayer many times the amount which it cost to conduct them. Criticisms which are aimed at governmental expenses, simply because they represent outgo, without considering the necessity for such expenditures and their ultimate worth, are too shallow to merit serious attention.

However, for the constructive critic who advocates more business in government there is everything to be said. It is a failure of our fiscal organization that from the beginning even to the present day both houses of Congress have found their contingent funds many times do not provide for investigations, yet they are ordered without the funds being in sight. Thereafter the expedient relied upon is either to raise the deficit through an emergency appropriation to supplement the contingent fund, or else to carry over the debt and meet it in later appropriations. Nothing short of that was the case in the report of the secretary of the Senate, cited above.

Moreover, there is a crying need, just as some far-seeing members have always recognized, of placing more strict limits upon the various items to be incurred during the investigation before the resolution is finally adopted. Many a hot debate has ensued over the simple question of whether witnesses in a projected investigation should receive three dollars instead of two, or vice versa. After a top price has been determined for the various items, moreover, adequate safeguards should be provided to see that the investigative budget is complied with.

A cursory study of investigations would probably lead one to ask, as is often demanded, why should abuses in the government be uncovered through the medium of investigations, when it is generaly known that little or nothing is done about it by Congress. The words " by Congress " bear stressing. For it is just this feature of the analysis that is almost invariably overlooked. The fact of the matter is that Congress usually does not have to do anything immediately. Corrective or criminal action is provided for in the regulations or dismissals of the executive, and in the laws provided therefore by which the courts entertain both criminal and civil prosecutions. It is an advantage of the system worthy of attention that Congress does not usually have to discipline or discharge erring officials. Its committees investigate, present the facts, and if the erring official does not resign of his own accord it is then a matter of responsibility for the President to intercede. Congress' function is fulfilled with having disclosed the fault, and by later, if necessary, enacting legislation to prevent the recurrence of maladjustments.

A final criticism of investigations has been touched upon above. It is frequently charged that an inquisitorial practice like investigations is irreconcilably opposed to democratic institutions. Investigations, it is pointed out, are not bound by any of the accepted rules of evidence. The constitutional rights of the individual are thereby transgressed. It is said that the investigative power is practically arbitrary, and that therefore abuses in its exercise are inevitable. Perhaps the only answer to this charge is the one suggested above. The courts have stated that so long as they have jurisdiction of this class of cases the citizen's rights will be upheld, and unnecessary searches and seizures will be forbidden. The courts invite more frequent appeals to their jurisdiction. Another thing which lessens the inquisitorial aspect of investigative procedure is that the committees themselves have constantly brought their rules of procedure more nearly into line with common law rules of evidence. There has been no relaxation of the unqualified demand of the committee for a complete exposure of information possessed by the witness, but there is a growing tendency to permit the witness an uninterrupted opportunity of presenting his side of the story.

Investigations and Public Opinion.—No consideration of investigations would be complete without reference to the effect of inquiries upon public opinion. Do investigations make much impression upon the voting public? To what extent are the exposures of investigations effectively applied to party campaign purposes?

The answer is that investigations do not influence voting to anywhere near the extent that one should expect. What was the situation with respect to the influence of investigations in 1924? This period is chosen because at no previous time were there so many scandals which apparently possessed a quality so damaging to the party in power.

The Democrats, with insurgent help, succeeded in setting at least a dozen investigations into motion as the campaign approached. They unquestionably thought that they were piling up a mountain of campaign material, but when they undertook to make use of it they found the data not nearly so valuable as they estimated. It is recognized of course that there is danger in attempting to judge the results of an election by any one factor, no matter how important that feature may appear.

However, it can be safely asserted that analysis of election returns by supporters of John W. Davis, the Democratic Presidential nominee, and Robert M. La Follette, who ran as an independent, revealed that the voters hardly had been moved by the disclosures in the Senate investigations.

One of the chief reasons accounting for this is that certain referents for the term " congressional investigation " have made the public openly antagonistic. Such referents are " fishing expedition," " party politics," " that legalized atrocity," and " scavenger of the private drains." This state of the public mind has risen chiefly from lack of knowledge of the practical significance of investigations. No doubt it is also due to the fact that almost without exception news reporters interpret every public event in terms of party and individual animosities. It sells papers. Add to these features of the situaton the fact that politics are generally considered sordid by nature, and that investigations many times drag out over a long period, thus wearying the reading public, and it is not surprising that, to most people, the mention of investigations is the occasion for jest and ridicule.

Probable Significance of Investigations in the Future.—As the final matter to be considered, some attempt should be made to forecast the future importance of investigations. It is thought that reference to the investigations undertaken, or which in all probability will be undertaken, by the Senate in 1928 is an indication of the future trend of inquiries.[4]

It seems unlikely that there will be any change in the present system of investigations concerning members, at least for many years. Even judicial hearings of election cases appear to be a remote possibility, because of the growing jealousy with which both Houses regard their privileges and powers. As suggested above, no device appears to the writer which would be preferable to the present system of investigating the behavior of members and infringements of their immunities and privileges.

The situation with regard to investigations as the basis of law-making is difficult to prophesy. There can be no question that the constantly growing tendency to extend congressional control over a wider field of social and industrial welfare will continue by leaps and bounds. Congress already has given administrative commissions broad power of investigation. However, since the tendency seems to be for the courts to re-

---

[4] By the middle of February, 1928, there had been three investigations concerning the membership of the Senate. These related to the qualifications of Messrs. Vare and Smith, and to charges that certain Senators had been bribed by the government of Mexico.

Investigations which are designed to aid law-making have been begun or are being considered in committee respecting public utility corporations, the tariff, the Pennsylvania coal fields, the issuance of labor injunctions, and the federal reserve system. A continuation of the Teapot Dome inquiry to determine what became of nearly three million dollars of the profits, may be declared valid by the courts in the Stewart case, on the ground of its providing material for future legislation. This seems questionable, however.

Finally, the executive and his subordinates have been subjected to investigation in relation to the S-4 disaster, and indications are that there will be investigations into the refunding of taxes by the Treasury Department and into the President's policy in regard to Nicaragua.

strict this power, it is likely that committees of Congress will have their hands full making investigations of the same character. This is proved, for example, by the proposed investigations of the public utilities and of the coal industry.

There is hardly any question but what Congress will establish additional administrative agencies, with investigative powers. In addition, commissions with power to take evidence for congressional committees in any part of the country will greatly facilitate the work of the Senate's own committees. The logical next step is the creation of commissions composed of congressional members and of experts, like the English Royal Commissions. The writer is inclined to believe that this development will take place, but that it will take several years to bring it about.

Investigations by Comptroller General Should Lessen Considerably the Number of Committee Investigations.—In view of the record of constuctive results achieved by investigations of the executive departments, one might conclude with good reason that it is unprofitable to consider possible measures of replacing such investigations by permanent instrumentalities. As a matter of fact, the writer believes that it is not only vain but also undesirable to make an effort to eliminate wholly investigations of the executive departments. For instance, in the case of investigations which accompany the impeaching process, and of those investigations of presidential elections it appears probable that at present no more preferable instrumentality could be found.

But we do not take this view of investigations which particularly concern financial matters, or those which are general investigations of the conduct and policy of officers in the executive departments. In these cases there are unquestionably permanent measures of control available which possess manifold advantages.

Viewed generally, there are two possibilities, or policies of permanent character, which might be adopted in bringing about a satisfactory supervision of the executive departments.

Mr. W. F. Willoughby demonstrates the two viewpoints clearly in his book on " Principles of Public Administration."

The two alternatives which Congress faces, says he, are minute specifications to all the departments in advance, or a requirement of full report of action taken. The latter plan is undoubtedly preferable. Mr. Willoughby's reasoning is so lucid that we shall quote this portion of his manuscript. After pointing out that heretofore Congress has resorted almost exclusively, in its permanent policy, to specifications in detail, he says:[5]

They have made this choice not because they have desired themselves to regulate details but because it has appeared to them as the only means of control.   Their fundamental mistake has been in failing to recognize the effectiveness of the control that might be exercised through the second method.   Until they have made effective means for control through such method, it is impracticable for them to abandon the first.   It is, thus, of the utmost importance that every effort should be concentrated upon the perfection of a system of accounting, reporting, and audit that will currently and automatically, as it were, furnish the legislature with precise and full information regarding the acts of all administrative officers and detailed data regarding administrative organization, procedure, conditions, and results of the work undertaken.   If to this is added a system under which the legislature will as a current part of its duties subject these data to careful scrutiny the latter body will find that opportunities for control thus offered will be far superior to those furnished by the attempt to specify action in advance. . . . By this means, and by this means alone, can it harmonize these two essential features of a proper administrative system-control and flexibility in action.

The establishment of an efficient system of budget and accounting, by the Good Budget Bill of 1921, goes a long way in the direction of such permanent and scientific control as Mr. Willoughby advocates. The executive heads were not slow to realize that the inauguration of the Comptroller General, not removable by the President as are purely administrative officers, would be taking a long stride toward lessening its discretionary powers and its claim as an equal to the legislative division. President Wilson peremptorily returned the original bill, stating as his reason that the proposal was

<hr />

[5] W. F. Willoughby, Principles of Public Administration, 34.

an unconstitutional limitation upon the powers of the President, because the act " undertakes to empower the Congress by concurrent resolution to remove an officer appointed by the President with the advice and consent of the Senate. "

Mr. W. F. Willoughby points out that the outstanding advantage in the Budget and Accounting Act as compared with the former system of accounting is that the Comptroller and his large corps are now in an independent position where fearless action is possible, and instead of merely auditing accounts, they actually control expenditures. [6] In other words, the Comptroller's counter-signature is necessary to signify that a particular requisition is legal and that there are Treasury funds to cover it.

But his prerogatives do not stop even there, for his powers are inquisitorial. This phase of his work is the most pertinent to our consideration of investigations by Congress. The Comptroller is specifically authorized to determine and report to Congress all cases of mismanagement or inefficiency, and any attempted contracts or expenditures contrary to law. In addition, the Comptroller General is expected to instruct Congress in ways and means of reorganization and distribution which would beget more efficient administration of divisions or departments. Then, in order to clothe its agent with sufficient resources, the act (Secs. 312, 313) specifies:

(b) He shall make such investigations and reports as shall be ordered by either House of Congress having jurisdiction over revenue, appropriations, or expenditures. The Comptroller General shall also, at the request of any such committee, direct assistants from his office to furnish the committee such aid and information as it shall request.

(c) All departments and establishments shall furnish to the Comptroller General such information regarding the powers, duties, activities, organization, financial transactions, and methods of business of their respective offices as he may from time to time require of them; and the Comptroller General, or any of his assistants or

---

[6] This subject is fully covered in W. F. Willoughby, The National Budget System. See also O. R. McGuire, " The Opinions of the Attorney General and the General Accounting Office," Georgetown Law Journal, XV, No. 2 (Jan. 1927), 115-127.

employees, when duly authorized by him, shall, for the purpose of securing such information, have access to and the right to examine any books, documents, or records of any such department or establishment.

It is not too bold a prophecy to suggest that such inquisitorial powers given to an agent of Congress should go far toward gaining administrative responsibility, and toward making more unnecessary extraordinary investigation by committees of Congress. However, investigations of the executive departments probably always will be numerous. A change to the responsible type of government is hardly conceivable. The jealousy between Congress and the President increases daily. No matter how satisfactory permanent devices of Congress for regulating administrative matters might become, there will always be the desire of the minority in Congress to investigate alleged inefficiencies and corrupt conspiracies by means of its own members, serving upon committees of investigation.

BIBLIOGRAPHY

PRINCIPAL REFERENCES

Annals of Congress, 1st to 18th Congresses (Gales & Seaton).
Congressional Debates, 18th to 25th Congresses (Gales & Seaton).
Congressional Globe, 23rd to 42nd Congresses (Blair & Rives).
Congressional Record, 43rd to 70th Congresses.
Galloway, George, "Investigative Function of Congress," Am. P. S. Rev., vol. 21, No. 1
Goodnow, F. J., Comparative Administrative Law, vol. 1, Div. 3, Chaps. 1 and 2.
Harvard Law Review, "The Power of Congress to subpoena witnesses for non-judicial investigations," Harv. Law Rev., vol. 38, 1924, p. 234 ff.
Hinds, A. C., Precedents of the House of Representatives, vols. 3 and 7.
House of Representatives, U. S., Reports of Commitees of (1820-1927).
Jefferson, Thomas, Manual of Parliamentary Practice for the Use of the Senate of the United States.
Landis, James M., "Constitutional Limitations on Congressional Power of Investigation," Harvard Law Rev., vol. 40, No. 2
Potts, C. S., "Power of Legislative Bodies to Punish for Contempt," 74 Penn. Law Rev., 691, 780 (1926).
Redlich, Joseph, Procedure of the House of Commons, 3 vols.
Rogers, Lindsay, The American Senate, chap. 6.
Senate, U. S., Reports of Committees.
Smith, H. H., Digest of Decisions and Precedents, 53rd Cong., 2nd sess., Sen. Misc. Doc., vol. 12.

SUPPLEMENTARY REFERENCES

Alexander, D. S., History and Procedure of Congress.
Bagehot, W., The English Constitution.
Burdick, C. K., The Law of the American Constitution.
Cleveland and Buck, The Budget and Responsible Government.
Constitution of the U. S., Revised and Annotated (1924), 68th Cong., 1st sess., Sen. Doc. No. 154, pp. 37-61.
Cooley, T. M., Constitutional Limitations, 8th edition.
Cushing, L. S., Legislative Practice.
Fairlie, J. A., National Administration in the United States.
Ford. H. J., Representative Government.
Frankfurter, Felix, "Hands off the Investigations," 38 New Republic, p. 329 (May 21, 1924).
Goodnow, Frank J., Politics and Administration.
———, Principles of the Administrative Law of the United States.
Hasbrouck, P. D., Party Government in the House of Representatives.
Jenks, J., "The Control of Administration by Congress," Amer. Rev. (Nov.-Dec., 1924).
Lowell, A. Lawrence, Greater European Governments.

Luce, Robert, Legislative Assemblies.
———, Legislative Procedure.
———, Congress.
McConachie, L. G., Congressional Committees.
May, Sir T. Erskine, Parliamentary Practice, 9th edition.
Munro, W. B., The Governments of Europe.
Oberholtzer, E. P., History of the United States since the Civil War, 2 vols.
Reinsch, Paul, American Legislatures and Legislative Methods.
Rhodes, J. F., History of the United States (1850-1877) vols. 6, 7, 8.
Willoughby, W. F., The Organization of the Administrative Branch of the National Government.
———, An introduction to the Study of the Government of Modern States.
———, The Legal Status and Functions of the General Accounting Office of the National Government.
———, The National Budget System.
Willoughby, W. F., W. W. Willoughby, S. M. Lindsay, The System of Financial Administration of Great Britain, Publications of Institute of Government Research, New York, 1917.
Willoughby, W. W., The American Constitutional System.
———, The Constitutional Law of the United States, 2 vols.
Wilson, Woodrow, Congressional Government.
———, Constitutional Government.

INDEX

Administrative commissions, investigations concerning, 113, 114.

Alaska purchase scandal, investigation concerning, 97, 98.

Alexander, D. S., History and Procedure of the House of Representatives, 163 n.

Anderson *vs.* Dunn, 53, 121-123.

Bagehot, Walter, The English Constitution, 12, 13, 37, 48.

Blount, Senator William, investigation of, 62 n.

Boyd *vs.* U. S., 158.

Briggs *vs.* Mackellar, 55, 56.

Brimson *vs.* I. C. C., 151 n.

Burdick, C. K., Law of the American Constitution, 59 n, 125, 126, 130 n.

Burton *vs.* U. S., 72 n.

Calhoun, Secretary of War, investigation of, 92, 93.

Chapman, *In Re*, 126-130.

Chinese coolie labor, investigation in respect to, 82 n.

Civil Service investigations, 112, 113.

Civil War, committee investigates conduct of, 111, 112.

Claims and contracts, inquiry in reference to, 96, 97.

Clayton Act, investigation prior to passage of, 81, 82.

Cohens *vs.* Virginia, 118, 119.

Colonies, investigations made use of in governments of, 53-55.

Commissions, supplementary fact-finding of, 82-84.

Conduct of government clerks, investigation of, 101, 102.

Congress, confusion of thought concerning the nature and functions of, 19, 20; its three functions, 20; relation to the Administration, 21-24; as a Board of Directors, 24-26; its use of investigations as a Board of Directors, 26-29; in-

vestigates its members, 57-71; use of investigations as collateral to the law-making function, 72-84; inquiries respecting the executive, 85-116. See also " Members of Congress " and " Law-making."

Corrupt combination of members of House, 64, 65.

Covode investigation, 109-111.

Credit Mobilier investigation, 115, 116.

Customs Service, investigations of, 93.

Daugherty, Secretary Harry M., investigation respecting, 30 n, 136-140. See also McGrain *vs.* Daugherty.

Deposit banks, investigation of, 107, 108.

Dietrich, Senator Charles, investigation concerning, 67, 68.

Dodge Commission, investigates Spanish-American War, 87 n.

Edwards-Crawford dispute, investigation of, 103.

Elections, presidential, investigation of, 114, 115.

Emden, Cecil S., Principles of British Constitutional Law, 34.

Executive division, attempted supervision of through investigative media, 85-116; the problem stated, 21-29, 85, 86; cases cited in which investigations of were conducted, 86-116; future of the problem, 172-175.

Federal Reserve System, investigations leading to, 81 n.

Federal Trade Commission, investigation prior to establishment of, 81, 82.

Federal Trade Commission vs. American Tobacco Co., 151 n.

France, provisions for investigations, 41; the interpellation, 40, 41.